Hynes, Jim; Lutes, Rob
TSN 25 Years: 25 years of hits and highlights, top tens and turning points through the lens of Canada's sports network / Jim Hynes, Rob Lutes.

ISBN 978-0-470-73648-7

1. Sports—Canada—History—20th century. 2. Sports—United States—History—20th century. 3. Sports—Canada—History—21st century.
4. Sports—United States—History—21st century. 5. TSN (Firm) —History.
I. Lutes, Rob, 1968- II. Title. III. Title: TSN twenty-five years.

GV742.3.H95 2009   796.097109'045   C2009-904206-1

Production Credits
Concept and design: Griffintown Media (Jim McRae, President; Annic Lavertu, Vice-President)
Cover and interior text design: Philippe Arnoldi, Art Director; Judy Coffin, Shanna Dupuis, Designers
Photo research: Saskia Brodeur, Chris Taylor and Jessica Park
Printer: Lehigh Phoenix

John Wiley & Sons Canada, Ltd.
6045 Freemont Blvd.
Mississauga, Ontario
L5R 4J3

Printed in the United States of America
1 2 3 4 5 LP 13 12 11 10 09

TSN 25 YEARS

25 Years of Hits and Highlights, Top Tens and Turning
Points, Through the Lens of Canada's Sports Network

Jim Hynes & Rob Lutes

John Wiley & Sons Canada, Ltd.

CONTENTS

A QUARTER-CENTURY OF MOMENTS

Sports and television make good teammates. They combine to captivate with unscripted drama, surprise with unexpected finishes and even console following unrealized dreams. And in the clutch, they hook up to deliver big plays that, given just the right context, instantly become great sports moments.

Sports fans have these moments etched in their memories, often recalling where they were when the last-second field goal won the game, the friends they were with when the overtime goal clinched the playoff series or the elation they felt when the rock stopped right on the button. Such is the passion of sport and the power of TV.

Canadians, in particular, can call upon a richness of memory and emotion that spans sports year-round — fitting for a four-season country like ours — as well as generations. In fact, so many moments in sports, captured with the immediacy of TV and shared simultaneously in millions of homes from coast to coast, take on a life of their own, leading to discussion and debate between both neighbours and strangers. It all helps to reinforce the collective persona of a sports-crazed nation.

The past 25 years have produced a stacked lineup of memorable sports moments, served up by a roster of heroes and stars, and sometimes just TV personalities, who add the personal element necessary for must-see TV. These players have become household names, and their exploits — so studied, shared and celebrated — have come to be referred to in code known only to the sports fan: The Catch, The Drive and even the Toe-in-the-Crease Goal are just a few cryptic examples.

It's been a quarter-century since TSN first brought the drama of sports to Canadians 24 hours a day, seven days a week. The past 25 years have delivered some of the greatest and most intriguing moments in sports history. The features and photos over the following pages will undoubtedly bring back a few memories and, with any luck, even lead to a debate or two. It's the sort of emotion that only good teammates can generate and share.

CHAPTER ONE

1984–1988

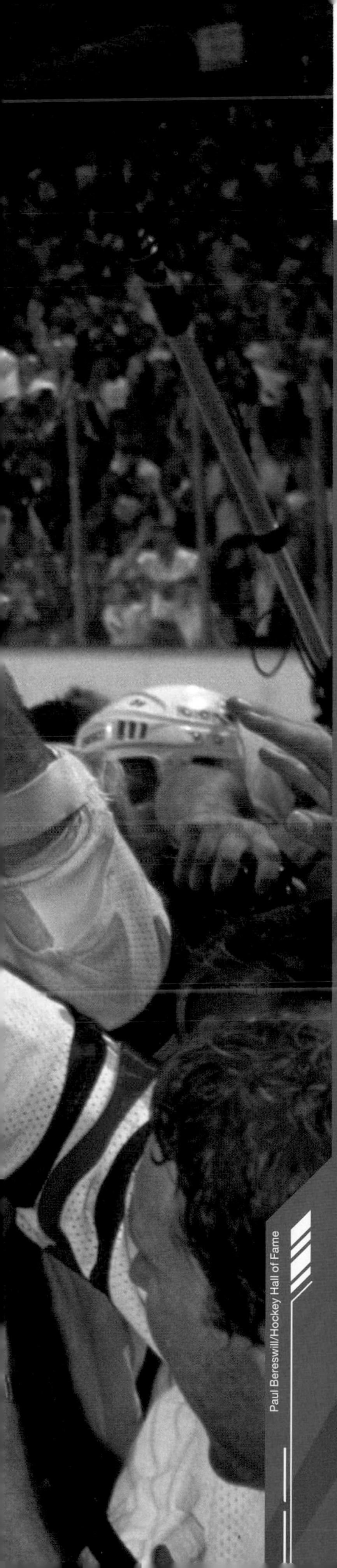

ON THE AIR

Like many of the great teams and athletes it would eventually spotlight, TSN had an enormous intangible in its favour when it launched in September 1984: clutch timing.

That year marked the beginning of a stellar era in Canadian sports. The Toronto Blue Jays, the network's flagship property, were poised to grab serious national attention with their first AL East title and playoff appearance in 1985. The Edmonton Oilers had just won their first Stanley Cup, kicking off a stretch of seven consecutive years with a Canadian team hoisting the Cup. Across the sports world, all-time greats Wayne Gretzky, Larry Bird, Joe Montana and John McEnroe were just entering their primes, while others, including Walter Payton, Kareem Abdul-Jabbar and Jack Nicklaus, were in the still-productive twilights of their careers.

The original TSN team — with some all-time greats of its own — brought the stories home to larger and larger audiences and silenced all the critics who said a Canadian all-sports network could never succeed.

Paul Bereswill/Hockey Hall of Fame

Wayne Gretzky was an iconic sports figure on Canadian television through the 1980s and '90s. He's shown here lifting the Stanley Cup in 1984.

1984

Boston College's Doug Flutie is lifted into the air in celebration after the game-winning

FLUTIE'S PRAYER IS ANSWERED

Hail Mary Curses Miami

It is regarded as one of the most memorable highlights in sports history. Before a sold-out Orange Bowl in Miami, the defending NCAA champion Miami Hurricanes are leading the 10th-ranked Boston College Eagles 45–41 with six seconds on the game clock. Eagles quarterback Doug Flutie, a shoo-in for the Heisman Trophy that year, drops back, eludes a tackle and unloads a last-second Hail Mary pass toward the Hurricanes' end zone.

The pass from Flutie travels 63 yards into 30-mile-an-hour winds, which is miraculous considering he has already thrown the ball 47 times in the game. The ball descends amid a clutch of players and, incredibly, is caught by wide receiver Gerard Phelan as he falls to the ground. Time has elapsed. The five-foot-nine Flutie doesn't see the catch and only knows it's a touchdown when he sees the referee's arms go up. Boston College players swarm Phelan in the end zone as Flutie is carried down the field by one of his linemen. Phelan later tells reporters, "I thought I was dead, but I was thinking to myself, 'What a way to go!'"

The game, which lasted three hours and 43 minutes, was an offensive gem, with both teams combining for 1273 yards and 15 scoring drives. With just 2:30 to go, the Hurricanes had trailed 41-38 and faced a third and 21 on their own 10-yard line. But quarterback Bernie Kosar completed a first-down pass to Darryl Oliver, and Miami went on to score, making it 45–41 with just 28 seconds remaining. "I thought we had won," Kosar later said. *Saturday Night Live* did a popular sketch of the Hail Mary play with Rich Hall as Flutie and Eddie Murphy as Bishop Desmond Tutu.

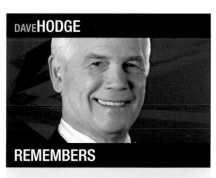

DAVE HODGE REMEMBERS

❝ It became the ultimate example of what is known as a Hail Mary. Obviously, the term was already in use at that time, but its use has probably become more widespread and more popular because of that play. And you know, the play became much more of a memorable football moment the day Doug Flutie arrived in Canada and we got to live it all over again. He did countless interviews during his time in Canada about that play, probably more than he would have wished to. ❞

Boston College/Collegiate Images/Getty Images

Hail Mary pass.

BOB McKENZIE

REMEMBERS

ROOKIE PHENOM MARIO LEMIEUX SCORES ON FIRST SHOT — ON FIRST NHL SHIFT

❝ At the draft that year, he refused to put the Pittsburgh Penguins sweater on after he was picked No. 1 overall. It occurred to me at the time that this was not your normal 18-year-old. I was kind of thinking to myself, "Well, you better be good." It turns out he was. He scored on his first shot of his first shift in his first NHL game and announced his arrival. That's all you needed to know about his talent and confidence. ❞

Allsport/Allsport

On October 11, Mario Lemieux announced his arrival in dramatic fashion, beating Boston goalie Pete Peeters to score on his first shift and his first shot on net in the NHL.

Team Canada captain Wayne Gretzky fights for a rebound with Soviet goaltender Vladimir Myshkin and defenceman Vladimir Zubkov during the 1984 Canada Cup semifinal.

Jimmy Lipa/Hockey Hall of Fame

CANADA CUP COMES HOME

Bossy Bags Overtime Winner

The 1984 Canadian team faced many questions as they prepared for the Canada Cup. With just five returning players from the 1981 squad and with Bryan Trottier crossing the border to play for the United States, many wondered whether the team would be able to erase the memory of the 8–1 dismantling at the hands of the Soviets in the 1981 final. The round robin didn't allay any of those fears. Canada finished with a disappointing 2–2–1 record, fourth behind the undefeated Soviet Union, a rejuvenated United States and Sweden.

The Canadians fought the Soviets to a gruelling 2–2 tie over the first 60 minutes of the semifinal and eked out a dramatic victory at 12:29 of overtime with Mike Bossy tipping a Paul Coffey shot past Vladimir Myshkin.

The Canada-Sweden final, a best-of-three affair, never approached the excitement of the semifinal. Sweden had more than their share of scoring punch with NHL stars such as Thomas Steen, Hakan Loob and Mats Naslund, but Canada rolled to an easy 5–2 win in the first game and took the second 6–5 for their second Canada Cup crown.

To no one's surprise, Wayne Gretzky led all scorers with 12 points in the tournament, but the Most Valuable Player award went to hard-working forward John Tonelli.

JIM VAN HORNE

REMEMBERS

❝ This was one of the first major events that TSN had the right to televise. I was the host, Roger Nielson was the colour commentator, and former NHL referee Bruce Hood was also working with us. Roger loved his dog Mike and he brought him with him to the studio every day. I still remember one incident where we were sitting there on the air and Roger was talking and all you could see was this dog's tail go by on the set. ❞

1985

JAYS WIN THE EAST
Toronto Takes the Next Step

The growing legion of Toronto Blue Jays fans across Canada got their first taste of glory in 1985. Coming off a second-place finish to the eventual World Series champion Detroit Tigers in 1984, the 1985 Jays rode a strong starting rotation, including American League earned-run-average leader Dave Stieb, excellent relief pitching and solid offensive production from the powerhouse outfield of George Bell, Jesse Barfield and Lloyd Moseby, to a franchise-best 99–62 record and the team's first AL East crown. Needing a win over the second-place New York Yankees on the final weekend of the season to clinch, the Jays — and their franchise-record number of fans — were rewarded on October 5 when Doyle Alexander's 17th win of the season punched the team's post-season ticket. After seizing a commanding 3–1 lead over the Kansas City Royals in the ALCS, the Jays dropped three straight games and the series to the eventual World Series champions. Ironically, it was the first year that the ALCS went to a seven-game format. Had it been a year earlier, the Jays would have made the Fall Classic. Toronto skipper Bobby Cox went on to win AL Manager of the Year, but he was gone before the 1986 season, replaced by coach Jimy Williams.

TV TOP 10 MOMENTS

1. George Bell makes the final out on a fly ball as Toronto defeats the New York Yankees 5–1 to clinch the Jays' first-ever division title.

2. Washington QB Joe Theismann's lower right leg is broken when he's sacked by New York Giant Lawrence Taylor.

3. St. Louis is three outs away from winning the World Series when umpire Don Denkinger calls a runner safe when he is actually out, opening the door for Kansas City to win Game 6 and then Game 7.

4. Toronto catcher Buck Martinez's leg is broken when he's run over by Seattle's Phil Bradley, but Martinez still records the out and another while lying on the ground.

5. At 17, Boris Becker becomes the youngest player — and first unseeded competitor — to win the Wimbledon men's singles title.

6. Cincinnati's Pete Rose cries and hugs his son at first base after becoming MLB's all-time hit leader with 4192.

7. Chicago lineman William "Refrigerator" Perry scores his first TD, as a running back, on a one-yard run vs. Green Bay.

8. Indiana coach Bobby Knight picks up a technical foul and responds by throwing a chair across the floor during a game vs. Purdue.

9. T.C. Chen surrenders a four-stroke lead in the fourth round of the U.S. Open when he double-hits a chip shot and cards a quadruple bogey.

10. Los Angeles wins the NBA final in Boston, ending an eight-series franchise losing streak vs. the Celtics.

ROD BLACK REMEMBERS

" The Blue Jays had for many years been this expansion franchise that nobody really talked about, but then in the mid-'80s it clicked with this band of great young players like George Bell, Lloyd Moseby, Jesse Barfield, Tony Fernandez and a great pitching staff. These guys were able to put it together and you could just see that this potential was going to be reached for these young players. I think a lot of people thought maybe "too much too soon." They were only eight years into their infancy as an expansion team and it happened. When that final ball was caught by George Bell, everybody remembers how it brought him down to his knees. It was one of those defining moments for Canadian baseball. The Jays maybe wouldn't have got to that 1992 World Series if they didn't do what they did in 1985. It began a culture of winning in Toronto. "

Dave Stieb led the 1985 Blue

Jays in innings pitched, ERA and strikeouts.

DAVE**HODGE**

REMEMBERS

PETE ROSE BECOMES MLB'S ALL-TIME HIT LEADER

  ❝ It was one of baseball's most cherished records, and so when Pete Rose broke it, it was a big occasion. But at the time, he was a manager and a player, so there were people who thought he was sort of hanging on as a player by means of his ability to put himself in the lineup as manager. Pete Rose was admired for the way he played, but there were things about his character that kept him from being as revered as he should have been or might have been. And then, of course, we remember that the record is not even officially recognized by baseball because of Pete Rose's banishment. And so it's a tarnished record. Not so much then, but certainly now. ❞

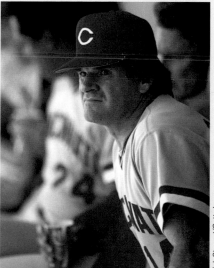

Rick Stewart/Getty Images

Pete Rose got his 4192nd career hit on September 11, 1985, passing the legendary Ty Cobb to become baseball's all-time leader.

LAKERS BREAK CELTIC CURSE

Lakers Rejoice on Garden Parquet

James Worthy averaged nearly 24 points per game during the finals, helping the Lakers finally topple the Celtics.

Rick Stewart/Stringer/Getty Images Sport

It seemed inevitable that the 1984–85 NBA season would end in a rematch between the Celtics and Lakers. Driven by the bitter taste of their seven-game series defeat to Boston the year before, Los Angeles had won 62 games that season and made quick work of Phoenix, Portland and Denver on their way to a return engagement. For their part, the Celtics won a league-best 63 games, with Larry Bird having his best season ever, and easily dispatched the Cavaliers, Pistons and 76ers to reach the championship series. In eight NBA finals matchups, Los Angeles had never defeated Boston, and the sting of the 1984 loss was compounded by the fact that the Lakers felt they gave the series away.

Riding the skyhook of 38-year-old Kareem Abdul-Jabbar and inspired play at both ends by a re-energized James Worthy, the Lakers rebounded from a horrific 148–114 loss in Game 1 to take the series in six games, clinching the title on the parquet floor of Boston Garden. The series was the second of five straight Celtics-Lakers NBA Finals, three of which went to Los Angeles.

ROD SMITH REMEMBERS

❝ I think the most important thing about that was it was validation for the Los Angeles Lakers as one of the great teams in NBA history. They had won NBA championships before but they had never done it against the mighty Boston Celtics. The negative distinction for the Lakers was that they had never beaten their arch rivals when it mattered most, in an NBA championship, and finally in 1985 they did it in six games. This was after they lost Game 1, one of the most lopsided games in finals history, by 34 points. They were led by the Big 3, Kareem Abdul-Jabbar, James Worthy and Magic Johnson, but this is one that they relied on Kareem the most. He bounced back after that ugly opening-game loss with 30 points and 17 rebounds. He had the patented skyhook, the unstoppable shot that was his trademark and one of the things that defined the Lakers of that era. ❞

BORIS BECKER WINS WIMBLEDON AT 17

German Teen Stuns Tennis World

On every level, Boris Becker's 1985 win at Wimbledon was one for the ages.

Becker was the first German, the first 17-year old and the first unseeded player ever to win the tournament, but it was the way he did it that made him an instant legend.

Becker earned his berth in Wimbledon after he won the Queen's Club Championships. His finals opponent, Johan Kriek, claimed Becker could win the coveted grass event if he maintained the same form.

After cruising to straight-set wins in the first two rounds, the young German had two close calls that could have stopped the incredible run in its tracks. Near defeat to Swede Joakim Nyström in the second round, Becker gained precious time to regroup when the match was postponed due to rain. In the next round against Tim Mayotte, Becker slipped, injured his leg and considered retiring from the match. Mayotte was too far from the net for Becker to offer his handshake that would have officially signalled the end. Instead, he carried on and won. Rain interruptions also aided the German in his semifinal win against Anders Jarryd. By that point, the entire tennis world had turned to watch the irrepressible teen.

Becker played with abandon, diving to make what seemed to be impossible shots and using his scorching serve and pure power to demoralize opponents. In the final, the outcome of which seemed somewhat of a foregone conclusion, Becker scored 21 aces and played half a set with his shirt caked in dirt from a spectacular dive as he defeated unheralded South African–born American Kevin Curran in four sets.

Becker would go on to win two more Wimbledon titles and add a U.S. Open and two Australian Opens to his collection. He reignited a love of tennis in Germany and became one of the sport's instantly recognizable superstars around the world.

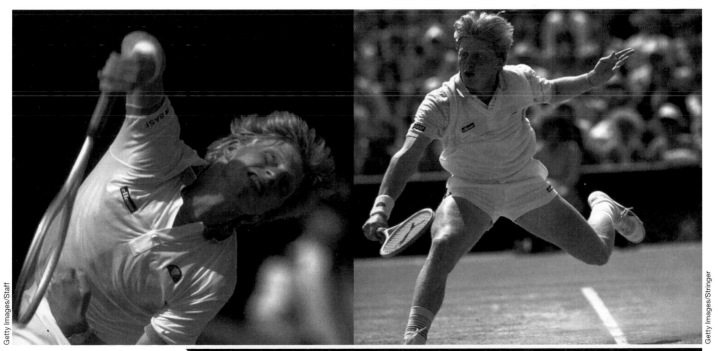

Getty Images/Staff

Getty Images/Stringer

Boris Becker's rare combination of power and agility earned him the 1985 Wimbledon crown.

1986

HABS HOIST CUP
Rookie Patrick Roy Steals the Show

Entering the 1986 Stanley Cup playoffs, the Montreal Canadiens didn't look like Stanley Cup contenders. The team finished the regular season in second place in the Adams Division and a full 32 points behind the President's Trophy–winning Edmonton Oilers. The Habs were a young team led by veterans Bob Gainey and Larry Robinson, the last members of the late-1970s dynasty. But as the team progressed deeper into the playoffs, another player was beginning to make Canadiens' fans believe once again. That player was rookie goalie Patrick Roy.

Like Ken Dryden had done in his rookie year of 1971, Roy played only part of the regular season before making his playoff debut. And like Dryden, his play was inspired. After sweeping the Boston Bruins away in Round 1, the Habs needed the dramatic Game 7 overtime winner from another rookie, Claude Lemieux, to eliminate the Hartford Whalers in the conference semifinal. That proved to be the team's toughest test as they rode Roy's stellar play between the pipes to five-game series wins over the New York Rangers and Calgary Flames to secure the franchise's 23rd Stanley Cup. To no one's surprise, and just as Dryden had done in his rookie campaign, Roy was awarded the Conn Smythe Trophy as the playoff MVP with an unbelievable 1.92 goals-against average and 15–5 playoff record.

MICHAEL **WHALEN** REMEMBERS

"I covered only the Montreal games during that series, and I made the biggest journalistic faux pas of my career. It was the day of Game 6 of the series in Calgary when then TSN executive Scott Moore called me and asked, "If the Canadiens win tonight in Calgary, do you think there'll be much celebrating in the streets of Montreal?" And I said, "Oh, I doubt it. I think they'll wait until the parade."

A friend of mine dropped by that night and said he heard that people were going crazy around the Forum. At the time I lived just a short distance from there so I said, "Well, let's go and check it out." And people were just going bonkers. As it turned out, there was rioting and looting throughout the downtown core of the city. Boy, did I call that one wrong, but learnt a lesson in the process. **"**

Canadiens forward

Claude Lemieux raises the Stanley Cup. The right winger scored 10 goals for Montreal during their playoff run.

Paul Bereswill/Hockey Hall of Fame

Allsport/Allsport

BUCKNER ERROR COSTS RED SOX DEARLY

Bill Buckner was an important part of the 1986 Boston Red Sox, and his .340 average, eight homers and 22 RBIs in September were a major reason they reached the World Series that season. He also had a critical ninth-inning single facing elimination against the Los Angeles Angels in Game 5 of the ALCS to kick off the ninth-inning rally that culminated in Dave Henderson's game-winning home run.

But his legacy was sealed on October 25 during Game 6 of the World Series. Holding a 3–2 lead in games over the New York Mets, the Red Sox took a two-run lead into the ninth inning with a chance to win the series. But three straight singles off Calvin Schiraldi followed by a wild pitch by Bob Stanley allowed the Mets to tie the game. Even with his injured knees, manager John McNamara left Buckner in. With the game tied, Mets centre fielder Mookie Wilson fouled off several pitches before hitting a slow roller to Buckner at first. It went through his legs, and Ray Knight scooted home with the game-winning run.

The Mets went on to win game seven and the World Series. To make matters worse, Buckner's error came after an 0-5 night at the plate.

Chicago Bears quarterback Jim McMahon scored two rushing touchdowns

Mike Powell/Getty Images

in Super Bowl XX.

DA' BEARS...

Chicago's Killer D Pounds Pats

The 1985 Chicago Bears were both a tremendous football team and a cultural icon. Not only possessing a smothering defence and a quality offensive attack sparked by Hall-of-Fame halfback Walter "Sweetness" Payton, the Bears also grabbed national attention with unorthodox characters such as mohawk-coifed quarterback Jim McMahon and 380-pound defensive end / running back William "Refrigerator" Perry. Led by coach Mike Ditka, the Bears rolled to a 15-1 regular season record.

By playoff time, their much-feared defence was hitting its devastating stride. The Bears recorded back-to-back playoff shutouts of the New York Giants and St. Louis Rams before dismantling the New England Patriots 46–10 in Super Bowl XX. The "Super Bowl Shuffle," the team's dance video recorded in the weeks after the game as a charity fundraiser, has a high cringe factor today but was embraced by fans at the time who adored the Bears' working-class ethic and team unity.

...AND THE BEAR

Jack Nicklaus Shoots 65 on Sunday to Win His Sixth Green Jacket

A short time after the Chicago Bears' win in January 1986, the Golden Bear, Jack Nicklaus, woke from a six-year hibernation to grab the sports spotlight with an unlikely and inspiring Masters championship. Ranked 160th on the PGA Tour money list going into the tournament, and not having won since 1980, Nicklaus, it was safe to say, was not considered an Augusta threat. But after three decent rounds, there he was at the turn on Sunday, trailing leader Seve Ballesteros by four shots. Over the final nine holes, Nicklaus — with the help of a roaring gallery — turned back the clock, making five birdies and an eagle to edge out Tom Kite and Greg Norman by a single stroke. It was the 18th — and probably most inspiring — major of his storied career. At 46, Nicklaus became the oldest champion in the history of the tournament.

David Cannon/Allsport

Jack Nicklaus acknowledges the emotional outpouring of Augusta fans after receiving his sixth green jacket from 1985 champion Bernhard Langer.

TSN CURLING SKINS

New Format Reinvigorates Old Game

In 1986, TSN broadcast its first Curling Skins game. In Curling Skins, instead of counting points cumulatively through games, teams capture skins by stealing a point or by scoring two or more points in an end with the hammer. Each skin is worth a dollar value, which is carried over if the skin is not won.

From 1986 to 2003, and in 2007 and 2009, TSN's Curling Skins Game has pitted the best curling teams against one another, fostering an ever-growing audience for a uniquely Canadian event. And like the popularity of the event, the money, too, has grown. In the inaugural TSN Skins, Ed Werenich won $16,000. In 2008, Randy Ferby walked away with $100,000. A women's skins event ran from 1996 to 2003.

2008 World Champion Kevin Martin, here at the 2008 Curling Skins Game, has won four TSN Skins titles (1997, 1998, 2004 and 2007) since its inception in 1986.

Courtesy of TSN

VIC**RAUTER**

REMEMBERS

❝ The first year TSN aired the Skins Game, we did it up in Newmarket, Ontario, in front of nobody. Ray Turnbull and I were doing the commentary and because there were so few people in the building, the players would wait for us to finish talking because they could hear us down the ice. And some of the Skins rules, including the free guard zone, have been adopted in the regular game to give it more offense. ❞

1987

JAYS LOSE IN LAST WEEK

Tigers Sweep Jays Out of AL East Title

John Cerutti enjoyed his best professional season in 1987, going 11-4 for the Jays as they battled Detroit down to the wire.

Rick Stewart/Getty Images

It was a pennant race for the ages. Between July 16 and September 25, the Toronto Blue Jays and Detroit Tigers, the two winningest teams in baseball, were never separated by more than one and a half games. And over the final 11 games of the season, with the Jays clutching a half-game division lead, the teams were set to face each other seven times.

After winning the first three in Toronto, the Jays seemed poised to cruise to their second pennant, but then some bad luck turned their prospects around. First, shortstop Tony Fernandez, in the middle of a career year that saw him bat .322 and win the Gold Glove, was knocked out for the rest of the season after a collision with Tigers' third baseman Bill Madlock. Five days later, catcher Ernie Whitt broke two ribs trying to take out Milwaukee Brewers second baseman Paul Molitor. Both had provided offensive punch and protection in the batting order for clean-up hitter George Bell.

Still, the Jays went into the final three-game series in Detroit with a one-game lead. Detroit's Doyle Alexander, a trade deadline pickup and former Jay, extended his Tigers record to 9–0, winning a 4–3 decision in the first game. With two to go, the teams were tied.

The Saturday game pitted two veterans, the Jays' Mike Flanagan against the Tigers' Jack Morris, in an amazing battle of attrition. Through 11 innings the game was locked at two. Morris had thrown 160 pitches before leaving after nine. Flanagan threw 147 — roughly 90 of them curve balls — and left after 11. After Jays rookie Jeff Musselman loaded the bases in the 12th, Alan Trammell hit a hard ground ball that bounced off Manny Lee's glove. The Tigers had taken the AL East lead.

The Sunday game belonged to Tigers screwballer Frank Tanana as he threw a masterful 1–0 shutout. In the end, the Tigers won the division by two games. All seven of the head-to-head matchups were decided by one run, four of them in the winning team's last at-bat.

The Tigers went on to lose the ALCS to the Minnesota Twins, the eventual World Series champs.

LEMIEUX AND GRETZKY MAKE MAGIC IN CANADA CUP

Dream Duo Leads Team Canada to Victory

Paul Bereswill/Hockey Hall of Fame

The offensive talents of Wayne Gretzky, Mark Messier and Mario Lemieux (above left to right) put fear into the hearts of opposing goaltenders. They combined for 15 goals and 46 points in the tournament.

GORD MILLER REMEMBERS

❝ I think that you had Gretzky at his absolute ascendancy along with Mario Lemieux. And, you know, the two of them together were just extraordinary. A lot of people think that that was hockey at its absolute best; that it was the greatest hockey ever played. And it's 6-5. The thing is that the score of all the great Canada-Soviet games is 6-5. The score of the Henderson game — Game 8 — and then the three games in that '87 Canada Cup final were all 6-5 and all extraordinary. Gretzky had five assists in Game 2 and considers that to be the greatest game he's ever played internationally. And, you know, the Soviet Union broke up after the '91 Canada Cup, so '87 was sort of the high-water mark of the Canada-Soviet rivalry. And it was also the height of those Soviet teams. You still had Larionov, Makarov, Krutov and all those great players. ❞

The 1987 Canada Cup offered up the tantalizing prospect of two of the game's greatest talents, Wayne Gretzky and Mario Lemieux, together on the same line. But as Team Canada finished the round-robin part of the tournament with a 3–3 tie against the Soviets, attention shifted to whether The Great One and Super Mario could create the magic needed for victory.

Canada sat atop the standings after round-robin play in the six-team tournament and advanced to a semifinal game against Czechoslovakia, which they dispatched 5–3 in come-from-behind fashion. The Soviets, second in the round robin, doubled Sweden — avenging a World Championship loss to the Swedes a year earlier — in the other semifinal. Hockey fans had what they wanted: a Canada-Soviet final. They wouldn't be disappointed.

In Game 1 of the best-of-three final, forward Alexander Semak silenced the Montreal Forum crowd with the overtime winner in a 6–5 Soviet victory. Game 2 was settled by an identical score, but this time it was Lemieux, on a pass from Gretzky, who notched the winning goal. The table was set for one of the most thrilling games — and moments — in Canadian hockey history.

Tied 5–5 with under two minutes remaining, Lemieux grabbed the puck off a Dale Hawerchuk faceoff win in the Canadian zone and rushed up the left boards, feeding it ahead to Gretzky as they headed up ice. Gretzky floated into the zone before feathering a pass back to Lemieux, who roofed a shot over the glove of Soviet goalie Sergei Mylnikov to seal the victory, sending the crowd at Copps Coliseum in Hamilton and fans across Canada into a frenzy.

Lemieux set a tournament record with 11 goals. His 18 points were three behind Gretzky's 21. To this day, many fans remember that three-game final fondly as the best hockey ever played.

Denver Bronco John Elway won the only NFL MVP award of his career for the 1987 season.

George Rose/Getty Images

ELWAY ORCHESTRATES THE DRIVE

Bronco QB Leads Game-Tying Comeback

Quarterback John Elway's ability to come through in the crunch was never so evident as in the closing minutes of the American Football Conference Championship Game in 1987. In a sequence of 15 plays over less than five and a half minutes that has come to be known simply as "The Drive," Elway cemented his reputation as one of the greatest clutch players of all time.

Trailing the Cleveland Browns 20–13, the Denver Broncos were pinned on their own two-yard line with 5:32 remaining. With incredible efficiency, Elway marched the team down the field, completing six passes and scrambling for 20 yards. On the Browns' five-yard line with 39 seconds left in the game, Elway fired a bullet to receiver Mark Jackson in the end zone to make the score 20–19. Kicker Rich Karlis nailed the single point to tie the game with 31 seconds remaining. But Elway had more work to do. On the Broncos' first possession in overtime, he promptly marched the team 60 yards to set up Karlis's game-winning field goal and earn the Broncos a trip to Super Bowl XXII.

The Broncos would go on to lose the Super Bowl to the Washington Redskins. Over his career, Elway led 40 game-winning drives along with seven game-tying ones, but none is as famous as "The Drive." He would go on to lead the team to back-to-back Super Bowls in 1997 and 1998, capturing the MVP award for the latter game.

GREY CUP RUNNETH OVER WITH DRAMA

Last-Second Field Goal Lifts Eskimos

On November 19, Vancouver's BC Place was busting at the seams with 59,478 football fans, each one lucky enough to witness arguably the greatest Grey Cup in CFL history. The Toronto Argonauts and Edmonton Eskimos exchanged leads five times, offered up a host of unexpected heroes and ultimately decided things with a last-second field goal.

The tone was set early when Eskimo Henry "Gizmo" Williams ran a missed field goal back a Grey Cup–record 115 yards for a touchdown. The Argos stormed back with two touchdowns by fullback Gill Fenerty, the first on a 61-yard rush. When Doug Landry ran a fumble recovery in for another score, Toronto had a commanding 24–10 lead. The situation for Edmonton got worse when quarterback Matt Dunigan suffered an injury that forced him from the game. But the Eskimos were far from finished, and if the team needed a positive sign, they got it with a blocked Argo punt and a six-yard touchdown pass from third-year backup quarterback Damon Allen to make the score 24–17 at halftime.

A low-scoring third quarter, 4–3 Edmonton, was followed early in the fourth with another Allen touchdown pass that saw the Eskimos retake the lead, 28–27. Toronto kicker Lance Chomyc put his club back in front by two with a field goal, but containing Allen was proving impossible for the Argo defence, and the athletic quarterback rushed for a 17-yard score to put the Esks up by five with just 6:39 to go.

There was more drama to come. This time, it was Argos quarterback Gilbert Renfroe who went out with a knee injury. His replacement, backup Danny Barrett, promptly rushed for a 25-yard major, giving Toronto a 36–35 lead with just 2:43 left. A two-point conversion failed, leaving the door open for Jerry Kauric to kick a last-second, 49-yard field goal to give Edmonton the dramatic victory.

Allen, the younger brother of NFL Hall of Famer Marcus Allen, was named Outstanding Offensive Player of the Game. He went on to play 20 more seasons in the CFL, ending as the all-time passing leader with 72,381 yards.

MICHAEL LANDSBERG

REMEMBERS

❝ A guy that I admire a lot, Matt Dunigan, got knocked out of that game, and a guy I also admire, Damon Allen, came in and beat the Argonauts. Allen came off the bench and with a change of pace, different look and different style, he changed the game 100 per cent. It all came down to the 47-yard field goal by Jerry Kauric, but the story of the game was when the Eskimos' No. 1 quarterback was replaced by their No. 2 quarterback. ❞

Kicker Jerry Kauric accounted for
Kauric was the top

14 of the Eskimos' 38 points in the 75th Grey Cup, including this last-second 49-yard field goal to seal the win. A Windsor, ON, native, scorer in the West Division in 1989 and played the 1990 season for the NFL's Cleveland Browns.

1988

Canadian Ben Johnson beat American rival Carl Lewis in the Olympic 100 metres only to relinquish the gold to Lewis two days later.

Romeo Gacad/AFP/Getty Images

JOHNSON DOPING DASHES NATIONAL PRIDE

Canadian Sprinter is Stripped of 100-Metre Gold

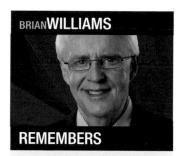

BRIAN**WILLIAMS**

REMEMBERS

Not all stories from Seoul were heartbreakers: Canadian super-heavyweight Lennox Lewis TKO'd American Riddick Bowe to win the gold medal. Lewis then went on to become the World Heavyweight Champion in 1993.

Courtesy of Allsport UK/Allsport

When Ben Johnson captured gold in the 100 metres at the Seoul 1988 Olympic Summer Games, Canadians rejoiced. The Toronto-based runner had not only bested his arch-rival Carl Lewis, he had done so in a new world– and Olympic–record time, a blistering 9.79 seconds. It was sweet revenge for Johnson. Lewis had been an outspoken critic of the sprinter, and as recently as June of that year, after beating Johnson at a Paris meet, the American told the media: "I will never again lose to John-son." Lewis had also openly suggested that Johnson used steroids.

Media lavished praise on Johnson, as the already celebrated runner was ordained a Canadian hero. It would all come crumbling down.

Two days after the Olympic win, the bombshell dropped and Canadian pride turned to shame. Johnson, it was reported, had tested positive for the steroid Stanozolol. Though Johnson denied he had used steroids, he was stripped of the gold medal, which was then awarded to Lewis, who had finished second.

Unprecedented national soul-searching ensued. Newspapers devoted pages to the story every day in the week following the revelation, so much so that the Canadian Press named the sprinter Newsmaker of the Year for 1988. The media, the sports world, indeed all Canadians wanted to understand how this could have happened. In response, the Canadian government launched the Dubin Inquiry the following year. Testifying at the hearings, which were televised live by TSN, Johnson admitted that he had used steroids since 1981. But the story was not quite complete.

Johnson made a comeback in 1991 and joined the Canadian Olympic Team for the 100 metres at the Barcelona 1992 Olympic Summer Games but failed to qualify for the final. In January 1993, at a race in Montreal, he was again found guilty of doping. The International Association of Athletics Federations (IAAF) imposed a lifetime ban on Johnson, effectively ending his athletic career.

❝ The build-up to the race was unbelievable. It was the marquee event of the Games and remember, no Canadian had won the men's 100 since Vancouver's Percy Williams in 1928. Even on the other side of the world we sensed the pride and elation felt from coast to coast back home. Three days later I was awakened in the middle of the night to the news there had been a positive drug test and I was off to the studio. Sports broadcasting came of age and displayed real journalism as CBC stayed with the developing story instead of going to live event coverage. When I got off the air I could barely lift my arms, as the tension and the pressure was overwhelming as we were flying by the seat of our pants.

The positive test unfortunately overshadowed two of the great Canadian performances in Olympic history. Dave Steen won Canada's first ever medal in the decathlon (a bronze) and Lennox Lewis won gold in boxing — Canada's first boxing gold since 1932. The cloud of 1988 extended well beyond Seoul as Donovan Bailey never received the proper recognition he deserved for his gold medal in Atlanta eight years later. ❞

CALGARY 1988 OLYMPIC WINTER GAMES

Jamaican Bobsledders Provide One of Many Olympic Feel-Good Stories

George Gobet/AFP/Getty Images

On the second day of competition, the Jamaican bobsled team achieved the seventh-fastest start time but crashed spectacularly later in the run.

The third time was the charm for Calgary. After failing with Olympic bids in 1964 and 1968, the city finally won the right to host the Calgary 1988 Olympic Winter Games. Canada's biggest gold-medal hope probably hung on figure skater Brian Orser, the defending men's world champion and Canada's flag bearer for the opening ceremonies.

In a showdown that came to be known as the "Battle of the Brians," Orser and his rival, American Brian Boitano, finished the compulsory figures and short program in a virtual dead heat. Whoever won the long program would take the gold. It would be Boitano, who skated clean while Orser made two small mistakes. In the women's event, Canadian Elizabeth

Manley skated the long program of her life to edge out American Debbie Thomas for silver, behind gold-medal winner West German Katarina Witt.

Heroes of the Games in Calgary included charismatic Italian skier Alberto Tomba, who won double gold in the slalom, and giant slalom and Finnish ski jumper Matti Nykänen, who became the first athlete to win three gold medals in ski jumping.

Two of the biggest stories, however, came from the unlikeliest of athletes. Ski jumper Michael "Eddie the Eagle" Edwards was a plasterer from Great Britain who had taken up the sport at the age of 22. He wore Coke-bottle glasses, had no funding and no coach and had broken just about every bone

in his body before finally qualifying for the Games just three months earlier. From his first jump, the crowds fell in love with him, dubbing him "Mr. Magoo." Edwards finished dead last in both ski jumping events, but he had become a cultural phenomenon and earned large sums for endorsements and speaking engagements following the Games.

Those who weren't watching Edwards were following the equally unlikely four-man bobsled team from sunny Jamaica. A group of American businessmen had noticed similarities between the bobsled event and pushcart derbies in Jamaica. They enlisted members of the Jamaican military to compete

in the Games. The team qualified in December 1987 and, despite losing a member to injury at the start of the Games, made two successful runs in Calgary before losing control and crashing in the third. The team walked the sled across the finish line to great applause from the crowd. The film *Cool Runnings* was based on the team's experience.

Despite the fact that Canada became just the second host country not to win a gold (the other was Yugoslavia), the Games were deemed a great success. Unlike the 1976 Olympic Summer Games in Montreal, with three levels of government contributing, the 1988 Winter Games actually turned a substantial profit.

↗ TURNING POINT

Getty Images/Staff

GREAT ONE TRADED

It was an event that shook the hockey world and reverberated through an entire nation. In Edmonton, it is sometimes remembered as the saddest day in hockey. On August 9, Wayne Gretzky, the greatest player in the game, fresh from leading the Oilers to their fourth Stanley Cup in five years,

was traded to the Los Angeles Kings in a five-player deal.

Though Gretzky was the focal point of the deal, the Oilers also sent Marty McSorley and Mike Krushelnyski to the Kings in exchange for Jimmy Carson, Martin Gélinas and three first-round draft picks. In addition, Kings owner Bruce McNall paid Oilers owner Peter Pocklington US $15 million for Gretzky.

As an event, Gretzky's tear-filled press conference was must-see viewing. His presence in L.A. immediately increased the visibility of the NHL in the United States and turned Kings home games into the place to be — and be seen — for Hollywood A-listers. But for Oilers fans, the bitter pill was not easy to swallow, made worse when during the following season Gretzky scored on his first shift in his first visit back to Edmonton. That spring, the Kings eliminated the Oilers in the first round of the NHL playoffs. And it was in Edmonton in October 1989 that The Great One broke Gordie Howe's longstanding NHL points record. But Edmonton fans would again have their day, as the Oilers would rebound by winning the Stanley Cup in 1990, something Gretzky never accomplished in L.A. despite reaching the final in 1993.

GORD MILLER

REMEMBERS

❝ People knew it was coming, but when it happened it was a huge blow to Edmonton. At the same time, it launched hockey in southern California and the southern states. It had a huge impact on the Los Angeles Kings and it expanded the footprint of hockey in the United States. Look at hockey's peak popularity in the U.S.: in '91 you had Mario Lemieux in the Stanley Cup final; in '92 Lemieux was in the final again; in '93 Gretzky faced off against Montreal, and in '94, the Rangers won it all. So it was a bright time for hockey and Gretzky was a big part of that. ❞

CHAPTER TWO

1989–1993

REAL LIFE. REAL DRAMA. REAL TV.

Skeptics be darned. Canadians, it seems, wanted to watch sports 24 hours a day after all. In 1989, only five years after its launch, TSN was in more than 5 million households. These were then joined by the 1.6 million homes in Quebec and Eastern Canada getting their sports fix *en français* with the launch of TSN's French-language counterpart RDS, *Le Réseau des sports*.

Back at TSN headquarters, the TSN family kept growing to meet the insatiable needs of its viewers and programmers. TSN's broadcasters were quickly becoming household names.

The Montreal Canadiens started and ended the 1989–93 period with a quest for their 24th Stanley Cup, and other Canadian NHL teams continued to contend for that ultimate prize. With the Toronto Blue Jays in their prime, baseball fever was at an all-time high in Canada. Meanwhile, a host of athletic heroes and villains — such as Wayne Gretzky, Magic Johnson, Michael Jordan, Mark Messier, Mario Lemieux, Patrick Roy, Ben Johnson, Mike Tyson and Pete Rose — turned each edition of *SportsDesk* into TV drama of the highest order on a daily basis. These were glory days, indeed, for Canadian sports fans.

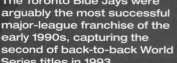

Rick Stewart/Stringer/Getty Images Sport

The Toronto Blue Jays were arguably the most successful major-league franchise of the early 1990s, capturing the second of back-to-back World Series titles in 1993.

1989

In an all-Canadian final in 1989, Lanny McDonald and the Calgary Flames downed the Montreal Canadiens and walked away from the famous Forum in Montreal with the Stanley Cup.

LANNY'S LEGACY

Flames Claim Cup on Montreal Forum Ice

The last final to feature two Canadian teams and a rematch of the 1986 final, the 1989 Stanley Cup final pitted the two best teams in the league against each other: the Campbell Conference champion Calgary Flames, who were still seeking their first Stanley Cup, and the Prince of Wales champion Montreal Canadiens, who wanted their 24th.

The Flames led the NHL with 117 points that year, with the Canadiens just two points off the pace at 115. The teams featured their share of NHL all-time greats, including All-Star goalie Patrick Roy and defenceman Chris Chelios shoring up the Habs' defence and Joe Mullen (51-goal man), Doug Gilmour and Joe Nieuwendyk bringing the offence for the Flames. They also boasted Al MacInnis and his cannon on the point, rookie firebrand Theoren Fleury and veteran Lanny McDonald.

It had already been a season to remember for McDonald, the Flames' 36-year-old co-captain. He notched his 1000th career point on March 7 and scored his 500th career goal two weeks later. McDonald, playing in his 18th, and what many believed would be his last, NHL season, had achieved almost everything a player could dream for in hockey. Almost.

The teams split the two opening games at Calgary's Saddledome, then headed to the legendary Forum in Montreal, where the Habs took a 2–1 lead on the strength of a 4–3 overtime win. But the determined Flames took the next two to set up a Game 6 back in Montreal with coach Terry Crisp's crew a win away from the ultimate prize.

The game was tied 1–1 early in the second when McDonald, flaming-red playoff beard now matching his trademark bushy moustache — and the Flames' road reds — joined a rush, took a cross-ice pass from Nieuwendyk and beat Roy with a glove-side wrist shot for his first goal of the playoffs. The teams traded goals again in the third before Gilmour's empty-netter clinched the win. The Flames had achieved what no visiting team before ever had: they won the Stanley Cup on Montreal Forum ice.

The disappointed Forum faithful nonetheless stood and cheered as McDonald and his teammates celebrated. McDonald, who had scored his first NHL goal at the Forum in 1973, decided to make this latest goal in the building his last and announced his retirement shortly after the game.

TERESA KRUZE
REMEMBERS

❝ I was the Calgary sports reporter for TSN in the late eighties and I remember the Flames were like a locomotive gaining steam throughout the 1988-89 season. They kept winning and winning and the momentum that they gained as the season and playoffs went on was just unbelievable.

After the Flames' Stanley Cup loss to Montreal in 1986, I remember Lanny McDonald coming out of the dressing room with huge tears streaming down his face. He promised Calgary fans that the Flames would get back to the Stanley Cup final again and win it. Three years later, there they were again, back in the Stanley Cup final with Calgary taking on Montreal. Lanny McDonald's goal in Game 6 was a phenomenal moment. I was covering fan reaction back in Calgary and Electric Avenue just exploded. Everybody loved Lanny, and we knew he was possibly playing the last NHL game of his stellar career. When the Flames' plane touched down in Calgary around 4:30 in the morning there were hundreds of fans all yelling and banging on the chain-link fence at the airport. The plane pulled right up to the fence. The door opened, and the first thing we saw was the Stanley Cup come out of the door. The look of sheer joy on Lanny McDonald's face along with the other Flames as they came down the steps with the Cup was amazing. And then to turn around and see the joy and pride of the fans in the middle of the night as they cheered their heroes home was a fabulous memory that I'll never, ever forget. **❞**

END OF THE INNOCENCE

Dubin Inquiry Exposes Steroid Use in Athletics

The Dubin Inquiry was called to get to the bottom of cheating in sports,
for which Ben Johnson had become the poster boy.

Don Emmert/AFP/Getty Images

The rumours and revelations that swirled following Canadian sprinter Ben Johnson's disqualification for steroid use at the 1988 Olympic Summer Games in Seoul forced the Canadian government to establish the Commission of Inquiry into the Use of Drugs and Banned Practices Intended to Increase Athletic Performance one year later.

Better known as the Dubin Inquiry — named after Charles Dubin, the Ontario Appeal Court Chief Justice who headed it up — the inquiry heard 119 witnesses over the course of its 91-day run, which was covered extensively by TSN. It produced more than 14,000 pages of testimony, much of it detailing rampant steroid use among Canadian amateur athletes. Ben Johnson himself, after pleading his innocence in the weeks following his humiliation, came clean to the inquiry, admitting that he had lied about taking steroids. His coach, Charlie Francis, testified that Johnson had been taking steroids since 1981 and, to his knowledge, 80 percent of Olympic track and field athletes used banned performance-enhancing drugs. Francis would later receive a lifetime ban from coaching in Canada.

The inquiry, which cost between $3-$4 million, issued its official report on June 26, 1990. It criticized the existing policies and testing procedures used by the Canadian government and amateur sports bodies and led to the establishment of the independent Canadian Anti-Doping Organization in 1991. The inquiry and the creation of the new body pushed Canada to the forefront in the battle against performance-enhancing drugs.

GREEN RIDERS WIN CLASSIC AT THE SKYDOME

Ridgway Kicks Last-Second Winner

Head coach John Gregory celebrates with the team following the Roughriders' thrilling Grey Cup victory.

The still-shiny and new SkyDome in Toronto was the scene of the 79th Grey Cup, a game that featured the return of the Saskatchewan Roughriders to the big show after a 12-year absence. Losers of that 1976 Cup to their Ottawa namesakes, the 1989 Green Riders weren't given much of a chance of coming out on top in this contest either. Their opponents, the 12-6 Hamilton Tiger-Cats, were heavily favoured to win.

The game was a veritable aerial show, with Hamilton quarterback Mike Kerrigan and Saskatchewan field general Kent Austin trading bombs that added up to almost 800 passing yards when all was said and done. Hamilton took an early 13-1 lead, but the Riders battled back. The key play for Saskatchewan was a 75-yard touchdown by slotback Jeff Fairholm that cut the Tiger-Cats lead to 20-15. When the whistle blew at halftime, Hamilton still led by five, 27-22.

The green and white took their first lead in the third quarter and still led by a touchdown (40-33) with under two minutes to play. But Kerrigan once again drove the Ticats downfield, where they tied the game after an acrobatic catch by receiver Tony Champion for his second TD of the contest.

With only 44 seconds left to play the Riders got the ball back and overtime seemed certain. That's when Austin went back to work, marching his troops to the Hamilton 28-yard line. With only nine seconds left on

the clock, the game was riding on the toe of Saskatchewan's Dave Ridgway, who had already kicked two field goals in the fourth quarter, including one that deflected in off an upright. Unshaken, even with a raucous, pro-Hamilton crowd raising the SkyDome roof, and a Ticat time-out intended to stiffen his leg and jar his nerves, Ridgway, one of the most reliable kickers in CFL history, sailed another one through, giving Saskatchewan its first Grey Cup in 23 years.

GLEN SUITOR

REMEMBERS

❝ When I look back on it, what I enjoyed most about that year was how we faced adversity. I don't think we had the most skill and at the end of the season, we were very close to not making the playoffs. But through that process, rather than point fingers and make excuses, we came together. We went into the Western Final against a 16-2 Edmonton team led by Tracy Ham that many were calling one of the best teams in CFL history. But we went into Commonwealth Stadium in Edmonton and beat them to get to the Grey Cup.

I was not nervous about the game-winning kick. Throughout my time as holder for Dave Ridgway, I always felt that he was going to make it. He may have been the best clutch kicker in CFL history. But that field goal was different. There were so many distractions. The Ti-Cats called a time out to ice him. The offensive line all of a sudden decided they wanted to become kicker coaches and they

were talking to him and telling him to keep his head down. So I was trying to keep the offensive line away from Dave so he could concentrate. I was managing so much of the huddle and stuff on the sidelines, I didn't really have a chance to get nervous and I just kneeled down and held the ball. As soon as he made contact I knew he was going to make it. ❞

Courtesy Canadian Football Hall of Fame and Museum

Mark Messier would put his stamp on the Edmonton Oilers after the loss of superstar captain

WINNING WITHOUT WAYNE

Oilers Capture Fifth Cup as Lights Go Out on Bruins

After Wayne Gretzky left Edmonton before the 1988–89 season, the Oilers' chances of winning another Stanley Cup anytime soon were thought to have gone south with him. When the Oilers, not even the best team in their own Smythe Division in 1989–90, did make it to the Stanley Cup final that year, they found them-selves playing underdog to their 1988 final opponents, and the NHL's best, the Boston Bruins.

The Oilers were led by new head coach John Muckler and captain Mark Messier, who, with 129 points (second to "The Great One"), was coming off his best season. The Bruins had the league's stingiest defence, anchored by

Wayne Gretzky, taking Edmonton to a Stanley Cup win.

KEN**CHILIBECK**

REMEMBERS

❝ I think it was the only Stanley Cup final that the Oilers went into as underdogs, because Gretzky was no longer there. I remember that they didn't have a whole lot of room for the media in Boston and we were squeezed into a little press box. When Game 1 went into overtime, I decided to go down to the media room, which is in the bowels of the Boston Garden, to watch it on TV. After the second overtime we were all kind of panicking because we had deadlines to get stuff back to TSN in Toronto and the game was dragging on and on. Then Klima of all people ended it.

Everyone remembers the classic picture of Mark Messier after the last game holding the Stanley Cup. But what I remember more was going back to Edmonton the next morning on their charter. I was close to the back of the plane with the players and Mark Messier had a seat right in the back row and here was the Stanley Cup in a seat like it was his little baby beside him. He put his hand over it and was holding it all the way back to Edmonton. That's what stands out in my mind — how important winning that Stanley Cup was for Mark Messier. Coming through without Gretzky was huge for him. That kind of took him into that next level. ❞

Ken Levine/Allsport

Norris Trophy winner Ray Bourque and backstopped by former Oilers goalie Andy Moog. They also had power forward Cam Neely and his 55 regular-season goals, and home-ice advantage. The Bruins could be punishing on the small Boston Garden ice.

In Game 1, Oilers goalie Bill Ranford, a former Bruin replacing the injured Grant Fuhr, was outstanding, and Edmonton clung to a 2–0 lead when Bourque struck twice in the third, the last with only 1:29 remaining. The game was going to overtime, where more hockey than anyone could imagine awaited.

Moog and Ranford traded saves early in overtime, but their workload diminished as the clock ticked on — and on. By the third extra period, exhaustion was setting in, alleviated briefly by a partial power failure that halted

play for 26 minutes. Three-quarters of the way through the period, Oiler Petr Klima, on for his first overtime shift, took a drop pass from Jari Kurri and guided a wrist shot past Moog after exactly 115 minutes and 13 seconds of play (stretched over six hours of real time). The Oilers celebration began at exactly 1:20 AM. It remains the longest Stanley Cup finals game ever played.

The Oilers hammered the devastated Bruins 7–2 in Game 2, won Game 4 at home and then easily finished them off in Game 5 back in Beantown. Edmonton ended up winning all three games played on the small ice surface usually dominated by the black and gold. Oilers goalie Bill Ranford won the Conn Smythe Trophy as playoff MVP, Craig Simpson led Edmonton with 16 postseason goals and Mark Messier led everywhere else.

TURNING POINT

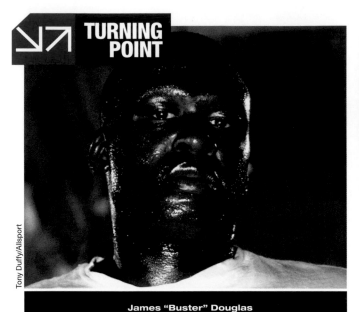

James "Buster" Douglas

"Iron Mike" Tyson

THE GREAT UPSET

James "Buster" Douglas Shocks Mike Tyson and Boxing World

DARREN DUTCHYSHEN

REMEMBERS

Japan's Tokyo Dome was nobody's first choice to host Mike Tyson's 10th defence of the heavyweight crown he first captured in 1986. It's just that none of the casinos in Las Vegas or Atlantic City had any interest in staging what was sure to be the slaughter of Columbus, Ohio's, James "Buster" Douglas.

Coming into the February 11th bout, Douglas wasn't exactly a punching bag. He had a record of 29 wins, four losses and one draw and had fought well in his only previous title bout, a 1987 loss to Tony Tucker. It was just that the unbeaten Tyson, in his fourth year as champ, had a habit of destroying just about everyone that dared to step into a ring with him.

But Douglas had a special weapon most people didn't know about — emotion. He had recently lost his mother and used her passing as motivation. Combining a 12-inch reach advantage, a five-inch height advantage and his newfound determination, Douglas started the fight strongly, landing left jabs and quick right hands that soon swelled Tyson's left eye. But even as Douglas continued peppering an increasingly sluggish Tyson, whose eye began to close completely, the sense remained that Tyson could, and would, end things with one punch. Near the end of the eighth round, he just about did, flooring Douglas with a right uppercut. But a dazed Douglas struggled to his feet at the count of nine and was literally saved by the bell.

Tyson tried but failed to end things in the ninth. The end came at 1:23 of the 10th, and when it did there was only stunned silence. Douglas unleashed a vicious right uppercut and then a pair of right-left combinations that sent Tyson to the canvas. The fight was over. David had slain Goliath.

Eight months later, Douglas failed in his first and only title defence against Evander Holyfield. Plagued by health problems, his career faded soon afterwards. Tyson, although he would be champion again, began a long downward spiral — on both sides of the ropes.

❝Tyson was such an intriguing individual. He was tearing apart the division, crushing everyone they put in front of him. And all of a sudden, Buster Douglas, a virtual nobody, beats him. It was an upset of gigantic proportions. Tyson was compelling at that time. There was a bloodlust when this guy came into the ring. It wasn't just that he beat his opponents. He was mercilessly crushing them. So it really was one of those "wow" moments where your response is "What? Are you kidding me? Tyson lost to Buster who?"**❞**

WOMEN'S HOCKEY DEBUTS ON THE WORLD STAGE

She Shoots, She Scores

An Olympic sport since 1998, women's hockey has come a long way in the past 20 years, drawing big crowds and TV audiences, especially for the dramatic matchups between Canada and the United States. But in Ottawa in March 1990, at the first Women's World Hockey Championship sanctioned by the International Ice Hockey Federation, few knew what to expect from the game. What would it look like? How would it compare to the men's game? Thanks in part to TSN broadcasting five tournament games, including the final, Canadians quickly learned to embrace women's hockey, and the women who wore the maple leaf.

If fans were skeptical at first, the pink and white jerseys worn by Team Canada probably didn't help. But after the first few games it became clear that the Canadian and U.S. teams, at least, could really play. Indeed, many fans came to find women's hockey just as entertaining as the men's game.

In the round robin, Canada dispatched Sweden 15–1, Japan and Germany 18–0 and 17–0 respectively, outscoring the opposition 50–1 overall. But there were good games too, notably a 5–4 U.S. win over Finland. The fans noticed. More than 9000 were on hand, many wearing pink, for Canada's dramatic 6–5 semifinal win over Finland to set up the first in what would be a long line of Championship finals against the United States.

The Americans grabbed a 2–0 lead late in the first period, but the Canadians stormed back with five unanswered goals, with the eventual winner by rookie rearguard Geraldine Heaney being a goal for the ages. Heaney, who would go on to become one of the best offensive blue liners in women's hockey history, joined the rush, deked a U.S. defender and, while airborne, put a high shot beyond the U.S. netminder. Visions of Bobby Orr . . . in pink. Hockey fans were smitten. Women's hockey was a smash hit.

Courtesy of Hockeycanada.ca

Susana Yuen scored midway through the third period of the final to give the Canadian team a two-goal lead over the U.S. When it was over, she was hoisted on her teammates' shoulders in celebration of the first-ever Women's World Hockey Championship.

CANADA'S PASTIME

Blue Jays Set Major League Attendance Record

I t's amazing what a spacious new home, and a winning team, can do for a baseball club's fortunes.

The Montreal Expos, who joined Major League Baseball in 1969, knew it to be true. With the exception of strike-shortened 1981, the team drew more than 2 million fans every year between 1979 and 1983, a period that more or less coincided with their move to Olympic Stadium in 1977 and five consecutive winning seasons.

The Toronto Blue Jays, now playing their first full season in the new SkyDome, were about to find out what a new, upscale home could do for them. The 1990 season saw the Jays combine strong pitching, timely hitting and a solid defence that helped them put together three separate six-game winning streaks, including two in September. On September 2, in Cleveland, pitcher Dave Stieb, the hard-luck hurler of five previous one-hitters, pitched the first no-hitter in team history. Back at the SkyDome, one sellout followed another. On September 19, 49,902 fans were on hand as the Blue Jays broke the Major League Baseball attendance record (established by the Los Angeles Dodgers in 1982). At the end of the 1990 season, the new record was 3,885,284. The Jays fell short on the field in the final week of the year, but baseball was suddenly Canada's pastime too. And in Toronto, the best was yet to come.

BUCK**MARTINEZ**

REMEMBERS

❝ Toronto fans had become very loyal, very quickly and with the Blue Jays getting better and better by the year, with the likes of Lloyd Moseby, Fred McGriff, Tony Fernandez and George Bell, there was a lot of excitement surrounding the team, especially leading up to the opening of the SkyDome in 1989. The following year, in the first full year in the new stadium, the team set the Major League Baseball attendance record and Blue Jays games were the place to be. It became a national thing. People from all across Canada bought into it, and even internationally, people were coming from all over the world to see the stadium because it was so unique. It had a lot to do with the development of the organization and with the way ballplayers, fans and other teams perceived the Blue Jays. People loved Exhibition Stadium, but the new ballpark brought the team into the Major Leagues. ❞

Rick Stewart/Stringer/Getty Images

The SkyDome was the limit when it came to attracting baseball — was among major-league leaders in attendance, drawing nearly

fans in 1990. From its opening, the state-of-the-art stadium — along with its famous tenants 4 million fans in 1990 alone.

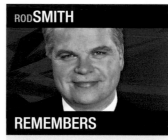

DAVE STIEB PITCHES BLUE JAYS' FIRST EVER NO-HITTER

❝ He was the best pitcher in Blue Jays' franchise history at the time and he had come so close on three occasions to getting the no-hitter — twice in 1988 he had no-hitters broken up with two outs in the ninth, and in 1989, he had a perfect game going into the ninth against the Yankees, which was broken up by Roberto Kelly. But the night he did it, his slider was biting perfectly and he looked absolutely untouchable. He was brilliant. People wondered, after coming so close, if he would ever do it. It was late in the season in 1990 at Municipal Stadium in Cleveland, in September, and Stieb no-hit the Indians and finally got it. I often wonder what was going through his mind when he had two outs in the ninth inning after all the disappointment that he'd gone through before. ❞

1991

1 Pittsburgh's Mario Lemieux makes a series of sensational moves to score a highlight-reel goal against Minnesota's Jon Casey in Game 2 of the Stanley Cup final.

2 Chicago's Michael Jordan puts an exclamation mark on his first NBA title, racing down the court for a one-handed windmill jam against Los Angeles in Game 5.

3 Vancouver's Rodney McCray runs through the right-field fence in Portland, Oregon, chasing down a fly ball in a Pacific Coast League game.

4 El Presidente, El Perfecto! Pitcher Dennis Martinez retires all 27 Los Angeles Dodgers he faces to record Montreal's only perfect game.

5 John Slaney scores the winner from the blue line late in the World Junior Championship final, as Canada claims gold over the Soviet Union.

6 With eight seconds remaining in the Super Bowl, Scott Norwood's 47-yard field goal attempt goes wide right and the New York Giants win 20–19 over Buffalo.

7 "Rocket" Ismail returns a kickoff 87 yards for a TD, helping Toronto to a Grey Cup win over Calgary.

8 Oakland's Rickey Henderson steals his record 939th base and says, "Lou Brock was a great base-stealer, but today I am the greatest of all time."

9 Texas great Nolan Ryan strikes out 16 Toronto Blue Jays on the way to a record seventh no-hitter, the final one of his career.

10 Magic Johnson announces he has tested positive for HIV and is retiring from Los Angeles and the NBA at 32.

In 1991, Los Angeles Laker Magic Johnson announced that his toughest opponent would no longer be found on the basketball court but in his life's battle fighting the HIV virus.

MAGIC STUNS FANS WITH HIV ANNOUNCEMENT

Basketball Legend Retires After Shocking Revelation

Stephen Dunn/Getty Images

Psychologists, amateur and otherwise, talk about a passion for sports as being a form of escapism. But sometimes there is no escape from life's harder realities. And sometimes a sports story is a big story . . . period. November 7, 1991, was such a day.

Los Angeles Lakers guard Earvin "Magic" Johnson, his famous No. 32 matching his age, was more than just a basketball player. Still in his playing prime, he was already one of his game's legends, a superstar on and off the court. But there he stood at a hastily convened press conference at L.A.'s Great Western Forum, one week before his 13th NBA season was to begin, calmly telling a jammed audience that he had the HIV virus, which can cause AIDS. The five-time NBA champion, nine-time All-Star, three-time MVP was announcing his retirement immediately

This was stunning news, reaching far beyond the sports pages to the front pages and the top of the evening news. There was sadness and there was fear. And there were so many questions. The disease was little understood and had a social stigma attached to it. How could Magic have it? The answer: anyone could get it, even sports heroes.

What stood out above the shock and confusion that day was Johnson's positive attitude and complete lack of self-pity.

"This is not like my life is over because it's not," he said. "I'm going to live on. Everything is still the same. I can work out. I'll just have to take medication and go on from there. I'm going to go on. I'm going to beat this, and I'm going to have fun."

Magic's words were no doubt chalked up to bravado by many in attendance and those listening around the world that memorable November day, but just like with the many challenges he faced on the court during his career, Magic prevailed, leading the United States to a gold medal at the 1992 Summer Olympic Games in Barcelona, Spain, and becoming a leading spokesperson for AIDS awareness.

MICHAEL**LANDSBERG**

REMEMBERS

❝ I remember listening to the news conference and my jaw dropped. I think those of us around at the time have come to forget how significant Magic Johnson was. He is arguably among the top five NBA players of all time. He started at centre in a finals game, and then moved to play point guard in the same game. No one has ever done that before, and no one ever will. He was phenomenal and he seemed like a super hero, and for him to be hit by something like that was totally unbelievable. It was one of the stories that had the greatest impact on me. Magic has since humanized HIV by making people aware that you could not only live and function with it, but even continue to excel in life. **❞**

A ROCKET LAUNCHES IN TORONTO

Argonauts Win the 79th Grey Cup

MATT DUNIGAN

REMEMBERS

" We had a much-needed influx of glitz, financial support and passion that year. Rocket Ismail was a young kid, fresh out of college, with a multi-million dollar contract to play and be the face of the Argonauts, a team that was already loaded with a tremendous amount of superstars. But nobody wanted to talk to us because they wanted him. It was just a tremendous setup. We'd go have fun and play football. We played that Grey Cup game in some of the most brutal conditions you can imagine, and with so many guys playing hurt. It was minus 19 and the winds were gusting. But Raghib continued to shine bright in the biggest of moments. That return for a touchdown was the final exclamation point for Raghib Ismail and that entire football team. It was a storybook ending to a storybook year. Hollywood came to Toronto. "

In 1991, Rocket Ismail nearly broke Pinball Clemons' Argonaut record for kickoff return yardage. He finished runner-up in CFL Rookie of the Year voting.

Courtesy Canadian Football Hall of Fame and Museum

When Raghib Ismael was signing his first pro contract in 1991, he was following the money as many do. The 1990 Heisman Trophy runner-up's choice of leagues, however, took everyone by surprise.

Ismail, the five-foot-ten, 175-pound receiver and kick-return specialist, rose to fame playing for Notre Dame, where his explosive speed and dazzling returns earned him the nickname "Rocket" and two appearances on the cover of *Sports Illustrated*. Ismail was projected to go first in the 1991 NFL draft, but at a time when the league's best position player, Jerry Rice, was earning under $800,000 a year, Ismail had other ideas. He shocked sports fans in the United States and Canada when he announced his intention to sign with the CFL's

Toronto Argonauts. Recently purchased by the "three amigos" ownership group of Los Angeles Kings owner Bruce McNall, Wayne Gretzky and actor John Candy, and newly installed at the SkyDome, the Argos wanted to make a bang. Rocket, who signed a four-year, $18.2-million contract, unheard of for pro football at that time, was their spark.

Ismail was an immediate success in Canada. He returned a kick 73 yards for a touchdown in his first game and helped lead the Argos to the Grey Cup against the Calgary Stampeders. Early in the fourth quarter of the championship game, with the Argos clinging to a 22–21 lead, Ismail returned a kick 87 yards for a major. The Argos claimed the Grey Cup and the Rocket was named MVP.

EL PRESIDENTE, EL PERFECTO

Montreal Expo Dennis Martinez Pitches a Perfect Game

On July 28, on a hot summer day at Dodger Stadium, the broadcast team of Dave Van Horne and Ken Singleton, calling the game on TSN, knew almost right away that Montreal pitcher Dennis Martinez had something special going on. Martinez, considered one of the National League's best pitchers, entered the game with an ERA of 2.05. It would be lower soon.

Singleton, a teammate of Martinez's with the Baltimore Orioles and the man who nicknamed the native Nicaraguan "El Presidente," told Van Horne that he had never seen Martinez work so effectively, keeping Dodger batters off-balance with his hard, sinking fastball and sharp curve and "painting the black" all afternoon.

By the fifth inning, Martinez had yet to give up a hit or walk. But Dodgers starter Mike Morgan was perfect too. It was a classic pitcher's duel under the California sun.

The Expos finally got to Morgan in the seventh inning, when Maple Ridge, B.C., native Larry Walker tripled with a full count, scoring Martinez, and later coming in to score on a groundout. Expos 2, Dodgers, 0. It would be just one of many zeroes on the Dodgers side of the scorecard.

With two out in the bottom of the ninth and the Dodger Stadium crowd on their feet in anticipation, L.A.'s Chris Gwynne hit a deep, towering fly to centre, one that Expo centre fielder Marquis Grissom pulled in to give Dennis Martinez the 13th perfect game in major-league history. As the ball disappeared into Grissom's glove, announcer Van Horne belted out: "El Presidente, El Perfecto!" — a call nearly as perfect as the achievement it described.

Dennis Martinez finished the 1991 season with a 14–11 record and a National League leading 2.39 ERA.

Gary Newkirk/Staff/Getty Images

DAVE VAN HORNE REMEMBERS

❝ It's not something that just came out on the final out. It was something that I thought of during the last commercial break before the bottom of the ninth inning. Dennis' nickname is, of course, El Presidente, and I had grown up listening to Phillies broadcasts in Pennsylvania and broadcasts out of New York, and I remembered announcers mentioning El Producto cigars as being a sponsor. And it just clicked with me. My mind was racing at the time, and El Presidente led to El Perfecto. And I thought, "If he pulls this off, that's what I'm going to say." ❞

A GREAT DAY FOR HOCKEY

A Stanley Cup for Pittsburgh Penguins Mario "the Magnificent" Lemieux and "Badger" Bob Johnson

By 1991, Mario Lemieux had already established himself as an NHL superstar. But his chances of ever winning a Stanley Cup on a Pittsburgh team that had missed the playoffs five times in his six-year NHL career were debatable. And when Mario "the Magnificent" started being plagued by back problems in 1990, that doubt was soon magnified.

The solid supporting cast the Penguins had provided Lemieux with at the latter end of the 1980s started to gel under new coach "Badger" Bob Johnson, he of the catchphrase "It's a great day for hockey." Young players like goalie Tom Barrasso, Kevin Stevens, Mark Recchi and 19-year-old rookie Jaromir Jagr skated alongside veterans like Bryan Trottier, Joe Mullen and Paul Coffey. Despite the absence of Lemieux, who missed the first 50 games of the season, the Penguins began looking like contenders, and mid-season trades for Larry Murphy, Ulf Samuelsson and Ron Francis made them serious ones, especially after Lemieux returned to notch 45 points in the season's final 26 games.

The surging Penguins reached the Stanley Cup final, where they encountered the NHL's new giant killers, the Minnesota North Stars, who took Game 1 at Pittsburgh's Mellon Arena. In Game 2, Lemieux scored arguably the greatest goal of his career. With the Penguins leading 2–1 late in the second period, Lemieux collected the puck in his own end and took off at top speed. Alone at the Minnesota blue line, he headed straight for the retreating North Stars defence pair, sliding the puck through the legs of a helpless Shawn Chambers before using his tremendous reach to slip a backhand behind goalie Jon Casey. The standing ovation seemed to go on forever.

Three games later, the Penguins dismantled the North Stars 8–0 to give Pittsburgh its first-ever Stanley Cup. With 16 goals and 28 assists, Lemieux was the top playoff scorer and Conn Smythe Trophy winner. The victory was a timely one, although nobody knew it yet. The Penguins would play for the Cup again, but their coach, the eternally positive Badger Bob, was stricken with cancer and died less than six months later.

Ken Levine/Staff/Getty Images

Mario was magnificent and unstoppable in the 1991 Stanley Cup run— his first and, sadly, coach Bob Johnson's last.

DARREN DUTCHYSHEN
REMEMBERS

❝ There was always this great debate as to who was better. Was it Gretzky or Lemieux? And this really was Mario Lemieux's ascension. Gretzky always had the Cups and at that time, Lemieux just had this ridiculous amount of talent. People were more in love with Gretzky. He was this good guy, while Mario didn't say a whole lot. He had been dismissive to Pittsburgh at the NHL draft. So you had this Gretzky camp and this Lemieux camp. But now all those who made the argument that he had no Cup, well, their argument no longer had any merit whatsoever. He was Mario Lemieux, Stanley Cup champion and still one of the greatest players ever to lace on skates. ❞

Canadian players celebrate John Slaney's World Junior winning goal.

Paul Bereswill/Hockey Hall of Fame

GORD**MILLER**

REMEMBERS

❝ What a lot of people don't remember about that time was that there was no gold-medal game. If the Soviets had beaten the Finns the night before, the Canada-Soviet game would not have meant anything. But the Finns managed a 4-4 tie. That meant the Canada-Soviet game was then for the gold medal. Chris Draper said recently to me, "I won the Stanley Cup four times. I've played in the Olympics, the World Championship, you name it, and that day remains one of the highlights of my hockey career."❞

NEW HOLIDAY TRADITION IS BORN

Team Canada Wins First TSN-Broadcast World Junior Championship

Apart from the 1978 tournament, the coming-out party for a 16-year-old Wayne Gretzky, and the 1987 event, which ended with the infamous "Punch-up in Piestany," the World Junior Championship (WJC) was not yet the juggernaut it is today. A little holiday hockey tournament, it was watched by few and usually won, at least at first, by the Soviet Union. That all changed in 1991.

For the first time, TSN owned the television rights to a WJC, held in Saskatoon, Saskatchewan. Team Canada was led for the second year by the bruising Eric Lindros, who was already a household name in Canada even though he had yet to play an NHL game. Fittingly, it all came down to a gold-medal matchup between Canada, the defending champs, and the Soviets, whose particularly powerful squad contained the likes of future NHL superstar Pavel Bure and a rock-solid defence that included Dmitri Yushkevich, Darius Kasparaitis, Sandis Ozolinsh and Boris Mironov.

All the Soviets needed — by virtue of a two-way tie with Canada atop the round-robin standings — was a tie to win gold. And that's exactly where the game appeared to be headed, deadlocked 2–2 with time running out, until a Canadian goal, scored on a long slapper by John Slaney, assisted by Kent Manderville, gave Canada a 3–2 win and the country's second consecutive gold. Thousands rejoiced in Saskatoon, as did nearly 1.5 million TV viewers, via TSN, in homes and bars across the country.

As of 2009, a total of 29 TSN World Junior Championship broadcasts topped more than 1 million viewers. Since the tournament debuted on the network in 1991, eight of the top 10 programs of all time on TSN have been World Junior broadcasts, including the 2009 edition of the event which was the most watched TSN broadcast of all time, drawing 3.7 million viewers as Canada took its fifth consecutive gold medal with a win over Sweden. This surpassed the previous high of 3.5 million viewers for the 2003 gold medal final.

1992

FLY THE FLAG

Blue Jays Bring World Series to Canada

There wasn't a Canadian in their lineup, but nobody cared. In most parts of the country, the Toronto Blue Jays were Canada's team. And for the first time ever, baseball's biggest showcase was heading north.

The Blue Jays had come close before, but a couple of trades and free agent signings made 1992 a banner year. Free agent slugger Dave Winfield and veteran pitcher Jack Morris were added in the off-season and proved to be good fits.

Toronto got off to a strong start and led the AL East with a 50–31 record at the All-Star break. The team faltered, going 14–16 in the dog days of August but rebounded brilliantly with a 21–9 record in the last five weeks of the season, helped by a deadline acquisition of National League strikeout leader David Cone. The Blue Jays staved off a late surge by the Baltimore Orioles and clinched their division at home on the second-to-last day of the season. The team had been there before and fallen short. But there was a feeling that things would be different this time around.

The Jays defeated the Oakland A's in the ALCS in six games, the key win being a come-from-behind, 7–6, 11-inning nail-biter in Game 4. The Blue Jays had finally won the pennant, and a Canadian team was off to the World Series.

The Blue Jays headed to Atlanta to face the powerful National League champion Atlanta Braves. Toronto dropped Game 1 but rebounded in what will be forever known as the "flag flap" game, where a Marine Corps honour guard flew the Canadian flag upside down, a diplomatic *faux pas* that garnered Canadians an apology from U.S. President George Bush. The two-run shot hit by Ed Sprague off reliever Jeff Reardon in the top of the ninth to put Toronto ahead 5–4 may be the second most-cherished home run in team history.

The Series came to Canada for the first time on October 20. In the fourth inning, Blue Jays centre fielder Devon White made one of the greatest catches in baseball history, scaling the outfield wall to snare a David Justice blast with two men aboard. The catch caught the Braves base runners off-guard, and only an umpiring error prevented Toronto from turning a rare World Series triple play. The Jays then got to Reardon again, eking out a 2–1 win on a Candy Maldonado single in the bottom of the ninth.

A Pat Borders homer in the third inning of Game 4 was the highlight of a 2–1 win. But the Braves rebounded in Game 5 and sent the series back to Atlanta. One of the most exciting games in World Series history saw the Braves avoid elimination, tying the game with two out in the bottom of the ninth. But the reprieve was temporary. A two-out, two-run double by Dave Winfield put Toronto up by two in the top of the 11th and needing only three outs to achieve a baseball first. Jimmy Key, on in relief, stumbled but got two outs, the latter scoring a Braves run that made the score 4–3. With two out and a runner on third, Blue Jays manager Cito Gaston called on reliever Mike Timlin, who'd made only one appearance in the Series. The batter, speedster Otis Nixon, attempted a bunt, which Timlin pounced on and calmly threw to Joe Carter at first base. Toronto — and Canada — had their first World Series title.

Just like the Canadian flag at one point in the World Series, many of the Jays were upside down in their on-field celebration of their first world championship.

ROD**BLACK**

REMEMBERS

❝ People always talk about the 1993 World Series and Joe Carter's home run, but I still maintain that if the Blue Jays didn't win in 1992, Joe Carter never would've got there in 1993.

My biggest memory of the '92 World Series was in Game 6 when the Blue Jays were in Atlanta and had the lead late. We were just sitting there in the locker room. They had already taped cellophane plastic over the top of the lockers because they expected a champagne shower in the room. And the next thing you know, Atlanta ties the game and we all get thrown out and they start ripping down the plastic. Then later, Dave Winfield gets the key hit for the Jays, they put the plastic back up again in there, and then the celebration ensues. It was absolute pandemonium. It was wonderful to see the relief, especially from people who had been with the franchise for such a long time. ❞

SILKEN'S COURAGE

Silken Laumann Captures Inspirational Bronze

The pre-Olympic slogan for some Canadian athletes going into Barcelona was "No pain, No Spain." It might have been written by Silken Laumann.

Laumann knew all about pain. Ten weeks before the Games, the 1991 world single skulls rowing champ and odds-on favourite to win gold in the event had her leg crushed in a rowing accident. She was told that she would probably never row competitively again. Ten weeks and five operations later, she went straight from a wheelchair to her skull to begin training for her Olympic dream again. And there she was, on August 2, awaiting the crack of the starter's pistol. Laumann rowed her heart out, incredibly upping her stroke rate from 38 to 40 over the final 100 metres, to capture bronze and the hearts of the millions of Canadians who'd been following her story. It was one of the greatest comebacks in Olympic history.

Laumann was an inspiration for the entire Olympic team, as Canada enjoyed their best performance in a non-boycotted Games, including seven gold medals and 18 overall. One performance stood above all the rest.

Canadian rower Silken Laumann personified the Olympic spirit with her inspirational medal performance at the Barcelona 1992 Summer Games.

Mike Powell/Allsport

TERESA KRUZE

REMEMBERS

"TSN broadcast the Henley Rowing Regatta in the summer of 1988. Silken Laumann had already won a bronze medal at the 1984 Olympics in doubles but now she was racing in single sculls.

Ten weeks before the 1992 Summer Games in Barcelona, I remember the shock in the newsroom when her shell collided with a men's pairs team during training. The collision had torn her leg apart and she was told by doctors she might not ever row again. She was the reigning world champion and was favoured to win gold in the Olympics and we knew if anybody could make a comeback, she could.

The day of the event, we were all gathered around the television and watched the race from Barcelona.

With a last-minute burst of energy and determination Silken crossed the finish line to win the bronze. It was an unbelievable comeback . . . one of the biggest comebacks in Canadian sporting history. On that day, it didn't matter that Silken hadn't won the gold medal. She made us all proud to be Canadian. She was our Golden Girl. "

ALBERTVILLE 1992 WINTER GAMES

Kerrin Lee-Gartner Grabs Gold

Kerrin Lee-Gartner grew up in Trail, B.C., the same hometown as 1968 gold medalist Nancy Greene.

Canada enjoyed a more or less typical Olympic performance at the 1992 Olympic Winter Games in Albertville, France. There were disappointments, but pleasant surprises too. Kurt Browning, arguably the best men's figure skater in the world since 1989, was dogged by a back injury and finished sixth. Pairs figure skaters Isabelle Brasseur and Lloyd Eisler, who had dreams of gold, settled for bronze. A new medal sport, short-track speed skating, was a bright spot for Canada. A then-unknown Myriam Bédard won bronze in the 15-kilometre biathlon, and the men's hockey team took silver, their best showing in 32 years.

But of all the Canadian performances, none helped re-instill Canadian national pride more than the one pulled off by 25-year-old skier Kerrin Lee-Gartner in the women's downhill on February 15, one week into the Games. Totally relaxed in the hours leading up to the race, she ultimately admitted to her start coach that she was nervous. "You should be," he laughed, "because it's the biggest race of your life."

He was right. And so was her timing. Skiing 12th on the bumpy Roc de Fer course that mercifully lacked the flat sections that were her weakness, Lee-Gartner pulled off the best run of her life. Second at the first and second intervals, with Katja Seizinger of Germany in first with a time of 1:52:67, Lee-Gartner reached for another gear and hit the finish line at 1:52:55. A number of the world's best followed her down the slopes, but none matched her incredible time.

BOB McKENZIE

REMEMBERS

❝ The main issue was the players' control of the rights to their own image, but it really had to do with Bob Goodenow, the head of the NHL Players Association, saying to the owners, "This is a new era." This was the first time in the modern history of the NHL that the players had gone on strike. It really was the coming-out party for Goodenow. He and the players were stepping up and doing something that, previously, would have been unheard of. And they did it at a time of the year when the stakes were the highest. If it had gone on a lot longer, the playoffs would have been in peril. The strike was probably the first tangible evidence that this was a new era and that the ground rules had changed completely. ❞

Paul Bereswill/Hockey Hall of Fame

NHL president John Ziegler struck a deal with the NHLPA, ending a 10-day player strike, but Ziegler was gone by the following year — ending a 15-year run as league leader.

DELAY OF GAME

Frustrated NHL Players Launch First Strike in League's 75-Year History

Other pro sports had walked the dark road of labour unrest, now it was the NHL's turn. On April 1, when the National Hockey League Players Association (NHLPA) announced that its members were striking, it was no joke, not for fans anyway. Coming so late in the season, the first work stoppage in the league's 75-year history had some wondering if the Stanley Cup playoffs could be saved.

Negotiations on a new collective bargaining agreement, the previous one having expired prior to the 1991–92 season, were going nowhere and would likely continue to stagnate as long as the games went on. So new NHLPA Executive Director Bob Goodenow proposed the bold move of going on strike late in the season. His members concurred,

and on April 1 they voted 560–4 in favour of a strike.

After a week of bad feelings, threats and missed deadlines, it seemed that the season would be lost after the union rejected the owners' "final offer" on April 7. The two sides finally came to an agreement on April 10, having resolved the key issue of trading-card revenues. The new deal left the players with more long-term security while the owners maintained some restrictions on free agency and got two more games tacked onto the regular season. The fans? Well, the playoffs would go on, but with only a two-year deal being signed, retroactive to the beginning of the season, they were left to wonder if they'd be going through it all again . . . soon.

Mike Powell/Allsport

QUEBEC NORDIQUES TRADE LINDROS

Former No. 1 Draft Pick Goes to Flyers

GINOREDA REMEMBERS

❝ This was a difficult situation for the league on multiple levels. To have a player saying, "I'm not going to go to this team" kind of dismantled the idea of the draft. If you're drafted first, you're supposed to go to the weaker teams. Then the league was embarrassed by the way the whole thing unfolded, with Lindros and the Nordiques engaging in what amounted to a huge public feud, which ended up with two teams thinking they got him. It was a comedy of errors from start to finish. ❞

The Eric Lindros story — which featured the best hockey prospect to come around in years snubbing the Quebec Nordiques, the team that drafted him first overall in the 1991 NHL Entry Draft — left few hockey fans indifferent. Some sided with the "Next One," as he was called, saying he shouldn't have to play where he didn't want to. Others viewed him negatively for refusing to play in Quebec.

Lindros was invited to try out for, and made, the 1991 Canada Cup squad. But when NHL camps started, Lindros stayed home. He later led Canada to a second consecutive World Junior title, helped Canada win a silver medal at the Winter Olympics and even returned to his junior team, the Oshawa Generals, for 13 games.

The struggling Nordiques, meanwhile, patiently waited for Lindros's stock to rise, and rise it did. One year after selecting him first overall, they finally traded him. But the Lindros saga didn't end there. Two teams, the New York Rangers and Philadelphia

Flyers, were both claiming the grand prize in the "Big E" sweepstakes. The saga went prime time again. The NHL hired arbitrator Larry Bertuzzi to make sense of the debacle. He had to decide who had the best claim to having officially consummated a trade with the Nordiques. On June 30, he did, stating that Philadelphia had "made an enforceable deal with Quebec." Lindros was a Flyer. Going the other way were seven players, including Peter Forsberg, two first-round draft picks and $15 million.

Lindros was an immediate success in Philly. And to rub salt into the wounds of Nordiques fans, he scored twice during his first game at Quebec's Colisée. The Nordiques, however, took the game 6–3. By 1996, the Nordiques had become the Colorado Avalanche and, with players acquired in the Lindros trade playing key roles, won the Stanley Cup. Plagued by concussions during the latter part of his four-team, 13-year NHL career, Lindros retired in 2008.

1993

WORKING OVERTIME

Saint Patrick Roy and the Montreal Canadiens Claim 24th Stanley Cup

TV TOP10 MOMENTS

1 Touch 'Em All, Joe! Joe Carter hits a three-run homer in the bottom of the ninth, giving Toronto an 8–6 win over Philadelphia and a second straight World Series.

2 Marty McSorley of Los Angeles is caught with an illegal stick late in Game 2 of the Stanley Cup final; Montreal ties the game on the power play and wins in overtime.

3 A crazed fan stabs Monica Seles in the back during a break between games in a Hamburg tennis tournament; Seles is treated for non-life-threatening injuries.

4 May Day, May Day! Brad May scores in overtime against Boston to clinch the Adams Division semifinal series for Buffalo.

5 Winnipeg's Teemu Selanne throws his glove in the air and shoots at it with his stick to celebrate his NHL rookie-record 54th goal.

6 Fan Man is attacked by fans after paragliding into the Riddick Bowe–Evander Holyfield fight and getting tied up in the top rope of the ring.

7 Leon Lett of Dallas runs for a TD in the Super Bowl but gets stripped of the ball by Buffalo's Don Beebe when he showboats before crossing the line.

8 A fly ball by Cleveland's Carlos Martinez bounces off Texas outfielder Jose Canseco's head and over the fence for a home run.

9 Robin Ventura of the Chicago White Sox charges the mound; Texas pitcher Nolan Ryan puts him in a headlock and punches the player 20 years his junior.

10 With 11 seconds left in the NCAA final and Michigan down by two points, Chris Webber calls a timeout; Michigan has none remaining and Carolina wins.

The 1993 Stanley Cup playoffs were marked by numerous upsets and a record 28 overtime games. When it was all over, the Stanley Cup celebrated its 100th birthday with some old and dear friends, the Montreal Canadiens.

In one of three playoff games in 1993, three periods would not be enough to determine a winner. And the masters of extra play that year proved to be the Canadiens. But what would be an overtime run for the ages did not get off to an auspicious start for the Habs, who blew a third-period lead and lost in overtime in the first game of their division semifinals against the Quebec Nordiques. Things looked grim for the Canadiens after a second loss to their provincial rivals, and collars were tight when the third game went to overtime. But Vincent Damphousse scored a controversial goal off a skate in overtime to put the Canadiens back in the series and start a remarkable streak for Montreal, one that not even the most wishful of thinkers could ever have dreamt up.

Thanks to another overtime win in the Nordiques series, the Habs disposed of Quebec in six games. Next up were the Buffalo Sabres, who were swept aside in four one-goal games, three of which went to overtime. Canadiens All-Star goaltender Patrick Roy was on a roll, with his legendary confidence at an all-time high. After regulation play, he would calmly tell his teammates to simply "go get one," stating matter-of-factly that nothing would get by him.

In the second game of the conference finals against the New York Islanders, the Canadiens needed double overtime before Stephan Lebeau blasted a slapper past the Islander Glenn Healy. Two days later, Guy Carbonneau's second overtime winner of the playoffs helped the Canadiens set a new record, with seven overtime wins in a single playoff year. And they were not done yet.

After beating the Islanders in five, the Canadiens faced Wayne Gretzky and the Los Angeles Kings, who had dashed the chances of a Habs-Leafs Cup showdown by beating Toronto in Game 7 of the Western Conference final. The Kings took Game 1 at the Montreal Forum and were on their way to a 2–0 series lead when desperate Montreal coach Jacques Demers asked for a stick measurement on the Kings' Marty McSorley late in the third period of Game 2. The stick was deemed illegal, and Montreal defenceman Eric Desjardins scored his second of the game on the ensuing power play to send the game to overtime, where his hat-trick goal won the game 51 seconds into the fourth frame.

The series headed back to Los Angeles for Games 3 and 4 . . . both won in overtime by Montreal, with John LeClair the hero each time. The Habs polished off the Kings at home in Game 5 by a 4–1 score. Roy was fittingly named the Conn Smythe Trophy winner. The only thing that didn't fit in this year of working overtime was that the final game ended in regulation time.

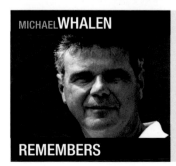

MICHAEL WHALEN REMEMBERS

❝ Reporters were allowed to travel with the team in those days, something that they are no longer allowed to do. It's a bit of a cliché you hear sometimes, players saying "We came together as a team," and I never really got a chance to feel that experience until those playoffs. You really got a sense as it progressed that the Habs players were willing to sacrifice themselves for the good of the team.

In the final series with Los Angeles, there was just this sense of purpose and focus that they all had. There was Gary Leeman down blocking shots, something that people would have been flabbergasted to see in his days with the Toronto Maple Leafs or Calgary Flames, the team he had come over from. It just seemed that if they went into overtime, they felt they had the opposition right where they wanted them. ❞

Stanley Cup goaltending hero Patrick Roy backstopped Montreal to a record 10 consecutive overtime victories.

GINO**REDA**

REMEMBERS

MARTY McSORLEY'S ILLEGAL STICK PENALTY IN GAME 2 OPENS DOOR FOR HABS

❝ Here was a guy who was doing what so many guys in the NHL do, and he got busted. It was a matter of being completely unlucky because so many other players have their 'game stick', and their 'end of the game stick'. The 'game stick' might have a bit of an extra curve on it or a skinnier blade because it gives a player better puck control, and it may or may not be legal. The 'end of the game' stick is legal because during the last five minutes of the game or overtime is when a coach may pull this kind of a call. McSorley got busted with his 'game stick' instead of his 'end of the game stick,' and it cost them the game. ❞

1993

TOUCH 'EM ALL, JOE!

Carter's Walk-Off Lifts Jays to World Series Repeat

Blue Jay Joe Carter launched a game- and Series-winning homer to dramatically bring Toronto its second title in as many years.

Rick Stewart/Allsport

A large hue and cry followed when the Toronto Blue Jays let veteran Dave Winfield walk away following their first World Series championship. But in the end, tears for Winfield would turn to cheers at the raucous Toronto SkyDome.

The Blue Jays filled Winfield's spot by signing veteran slugger Paul Molitor and speedster Rickey Henderson and also added All-Star Dave Stewart to the pitching rotation. They started the title defence slowly, but a 17–6 run in June helped put them back atop the AL East by the season's halfway mark. Led by the WAMCO of Devon White, Robbie Alomar, Paul Molitor, Joe Carter and first baseman John Olerud — who chased .400 into August before winning the batting title with a .363 average (ahead of Molitor and Alomar) — the Blue Jays easily captured the division title with a 95–67 record, seven games ahead of the second-place New York Yankees.

A six-game defeat of the Chicago White Sox put Toronto into the World Series for the second year in a row. Awaiting them were the rowdy NL champion Philadelphia Phillies.

After splitting the two opening games at the SkyDome, the teams headed to Philadelphia's Veterans Stadium for the next three. Game 3 was a 10–3 Toronto rout. But Game 4 was a wild roller-coaster ride, with scoring in every inning but the ninth. Philadelphia scored five times in the fifth to go up 12–7, but the Blue Jays refused to quit. Trailing 14–9 in the eighth, Toronto scored six times, a two-run triple by Devon White being the key hit. Toronto reliever Duane Ward closed the door on the game that set World Series records for length (four hours, 14 minutes), runs (29) and runs by a losing team.

The Phillies, without an ounce of quit in them either, took Game 5 at 2–0. The Series headed back to the SkyDome for Game 6, and Game 7 looked like a distinct possibility when the Phillies scored five runs in the seventh inning to grab a 6–5 lead. The Phillies trotted out their hard-throwing but unpredictable reliever Mitch "Wild Thing" Williams, who promptly walked Henderson on four pitches. Molitor followed a Devon White fly out with a sharp single that put two men on for Joe Carter,

the owner of 33 regular-season home runs. Carter had been having an unproductive Series, but not for long. With the count at 2–2, Carter drove Williams' next offering over the left-field wall to give the Jays the Series. It marked only the second time that a World Series ended on a home run. The pitch, the swing, announcer Tom Cheek's call — "Touch 'em all, Joe!" — and the wild celebration at home plate would all make for an instant Canadian sports classic.

DAVE HODGE REMEMBERS

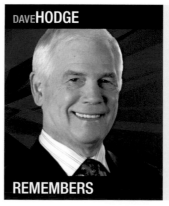

❝ I can remember Toronto fans being somewhat restrained then, and even now. But the SkyDome was in a complete uproar as the Blue Jays comeback was taking place. Just before the Joe Carter home run, I looked around and saw that literally all 50,000 people were on their feet, and I'm not sure I'd ever seen that before anywhere in Toronto. **❞**

MICHAEL JORDAN HANGS THEM UP

Jordan Retirement Shocks Sports World

JACK**ARMSTRONG**

REMEMBERS

❝ In my time watching athletes perform, I have never seen a more locked in, competitive, win-at-all-costs individual. So when I heard this news, I almost drove off the road. I knew about his father, but I still couldn't understand why this was happening. The two guys I thought of immediately were Jim Brown and Sandy Koufax: two guys who left in their prime.

The fact that he left to play baseball I thought was a bit bizarre. For a guy who is so driven and intense, baseball is not the sport you think of. After watching him play baseball, speaking to people that knew him, and knowing what kind of competitor that Michael Jordan was and is, I knew there was no way he wasn't going to come back. ❞

Jonathan Daniel/Stringer/Getty Images

"Air Jordan" is grounded — prematurely — as the Chicago hoops great announced his retirement in the prime of his career.

Few athletes have done more for their sport than Michael Jordan did for his. Jordan brought worldwide recognition to the NBA and the game of basketball. At one time, Bulls jerseys with his name on the back were as common at Madison Square Garden in New York City as they were in Piccadilly Square in London. The year 1993 had a typical Michael Jordan beginning, but a surprising ending.

At age 30, Jordan was at the top of his game: highest scoring average in NBA history, three-time MVP and, along with his Chicago Bulls, a three-peat winner of the NBA Championship. In beating Charles Barkley and the Phoenix Suns in the six-game final, "His Airness" ruled the basketball world. No one knew he was about to abdicate.

Rumours of Jordan's gambling habits led to an NBA investigation and led to his appearance in a different kind of court to testify against a noted gambler and convicted felon. His year would get worse.

In early August, the body of his father, James Jordan, was found in South Carolina, the victim of a random roadside robbery and murder. Michael not only lost his father, but his best friend, a man who'd been by his side for the biggest mo-

ments of his life. Basketball was suddenly the furthest thing from Michael Jordan's mind.

On October 6, Jordan shocked basketball fans by announcing his retirement, saying he had lost his motivation and had nothing left to prove in his sport. "It's time for me to move away from the game of basketball," he said.

Jordan would remain retired for two seasons, both non-title years for the Bulls, only to return for the start of the 1995-96 campaign to begin a second three-peat championship run, incredibly earning a second hat-trick of finals MVP awards along the way.

LEMIEUX ANNOUNCES HE HAS HODGKIN'S DISEASE

Penguins Superstar Receives Treatment and Returns to Capture Scoring Race

With 104 points in his first 40 games before being diagnosed with Hodgkins disease, Mario Lemieux was on pace to challenge Wayne Gretzky's record of 215 points in a season.

Robert Laberge/Staff/Getty Images

Opposing defences and goalies could not stop him. Only injuries could. But this was more than the chronic back pain Mario Lemieux was used to dealing with. This was a life-threatening illness. And suddenly the game was the least of anyone's concerns. It was not just about hockey anymore.

On January 12, the Pittsburgh Penguins superstar shocked the hockey world when he announced that he was suffering from Hodgkin's disease, a form of cancer. Lemieux learned of his illness after a biopsy was performed on a lump found on his neck during a back exam. Lemieux later admitted that after doctors informed him of their findings, he could barely drive home because of the tears in his eyes.

Doctors ordered four weeks of radiation treatment, saying Lemieux's chances of a full recovery were excellent. But Mario the Magnificent wasn't looking ahead to a return; he was concerned with beating the disease.

The day the treatment ended, Lemieux boarded a plane and rejoined the Penguins in Philadelphia. If there was any rust from the four-week layoff that caused him to miss 23 games, it didn't show. Lemieux picked up where he left off, scoring his 40th goal of the season and adding an assist in his first game back. Then he went on an absolute tear, scoring 52 points in the season's final 20 games. Trailing by 12 points in the scoring race at his return, he would go on to win by the same amount, tallying 69 times and adding 91 assists for a total of 160 points in only 60 games.

The Penguins wrapped up their season with a record 17-game winning streak. But with Lemieux's bad back acting up again, the defending champions suffered a shocking loss to the New York Islanders in the conference semifinal. At the NHL Awards ceremony in June, Lemieux collected his second career Hart Memorial Trophy as league MVP and the Bill Masterton Memorial Trophy for perseverance to go with the Art Ross Trophy he earned as the scoring champion. He was later awarded the Lionel Conacher Award as Canada's Male Athlete of the Year for 1993.

NORTHERN EXPOSURE

NBA Awards Franchise to Toronto

As the CFL headed south, adding a franchise in Sacramento, California, and announcing another for Las Vegas, the NBA headed north into Canada, with better, but still mixed, results.

The seed for NBA expansion was planted at the All-Star Game in February when Toronto's Palestra Group, led by Toronto construction magnate Larry Tanenbaum, submitted an unsolicited $100,000 franchise application fee. A few months later, with more Toronto groups showing interest, the NBA made the decision to expand outside the United States. In September, four Canadian groups made presentations to the NBA's expansion committee in New York City. Three strong Toronto bids were joined by another from Vancouver Canucks owner Arthur Griffiths, who wanted a team on Canada's West Coast. A Toronto franchise was awarded to the last group to present, led by Toronto businessman John Bitove.

On November 4, the NBA Board of Governors approved the bid. For $125 million, Toronto would have an NBA team. The league also announced that it would consider adding a team in Vancouver once the financing for its bid was in place, something that occurred early in 1994. Both teams debuted in 1995. The Toronto Raptors, despite ups and downs on the court, were an instant success. The Vancouver Grizzlies, on the other hand, didn't survive and moved to Memphis, Tennessee, in 2001.

Carlo Allegri/AFP/Getty Images

Raptors Executive Vice-President Isiah Thomas helps to unveil the Toronto Raptors logo. Thomas remained with the franchise until 1998, drafting Damon Stoudamire, Marcus Camby and Tracy McGrady, among others, during his tenure.

CHAPTER THREE

1994–1998

SEE IT. LIVE IT.

A spate of stories appeared in the mid-1990s that blurred the line between sports and hard news. Bizarre events, such as those involving football great O.J. Simpson and figure skater Tonya Harding, were discussed and debated as much in the general public as by sports fans.

Fortunately, the good news outweighed the bad. Hockey fans witnessed the happy end of two seemingly endless title droughts as the New York Rangers and the Detroit Red Wings both brought home the Stanley Cup. Baseball fans were able to engage their love of history as they watched one of the game's classiest players, Cal Ripken Jr., surpass the consecutive games record of another beloved legend, Lou Gehrig. Canadian race-car driver Jacques Villeneuve and sprinter Donovan Bailey gave winning performances that erased painful memories. And hockey fans in Montreal offered a sublime tribute to a living legend.

With coverage of major teams, athletes and sporting events from across Canada and the world, TSN continued to grow as a network. In 1995, it launched TSN.ca, an industry-leading website that quickly became Canada's online source for sporting news.

Don Emmert/AFP/Getty Images

Arguably the greatest moment in Canadian Olympic history was provided by Donovan Bailey and his dramatic 100-metre gold-medal sprint at the 1996 Olympic Summer Games in Atlanta.

1994

TV TOP10 MOMENTS

1 Football legend and suspected murderer O.J. Simpson leads the LAPD on a slow chase along Los Angeles freeways.

2 Nancy Kerrigan is hit on the knee with a metal baton by an associate of rival Tonya Harding at the U.S. Figure Skating Championship.

3 Los Angeles' Wayne Gretzky breaks Gordie Howe's career-goal mark by redirecting a pass into the Vancouver net for number 802.

4 Peter Forsberg scores on Canadian goalie Corey Hirsch with a brilliant fake in the shootout to win Olympic gold for Sweden.

5 Italy's Roberto Baggio sails the ball over the net in penalty kicks, giving Brazil the World Cup.

6 The New York Rangers win their first Stanley Cup in 54 years with a victory over Vancouver in Game 7.

7 B.C. wins the first-ever international Grey Cup, beating Baltimore 26–23.

8 Canadian Jean-Luc Brassard wins gold in moguls as freestyle skiing makes its debut at the Lillehammer 1994 Olympic Winter Games.

9 Andres Escobar's own goal in the World Cup leads to Colombia's exit. Escobar is murdered within two weeks.

10 George Foreman knocks out undefeated Michael Moorer to become the oldest heavyweight champion at 45.

"THE GREAT ONE" PASSES "MR. HOCKEY"

Wayne Gretzky Breaks Gordie Howe's Career-Goal Mark

Entering the 1993–94 NHL season, his 15th in the league, Wayne Gretzky had already put an indelible stamp on the record book. Among the many records in his possession were those for all-time points, as well as for goals, assists and points in a single season. There was just one mountain left to climb, the game's "unbreakable" record of 801 career goals set by Gordie Howe more than 30 years before.

Throughout the year, "The Great One" had inched closer and closer to the mark. On March 21, he scored twice against the San Jose Sharks to tie Howe at 801. Coming home for a March 23 tilt against the Vancouver Canucks with a chance to capture the most coveted record in the game, No. 99 once again had the eyes of the world firmly fixed upon his every shift.

There was an added dimension to this record chase for Gretzky, as he had idolized Howe growing up. "I respect Gordie so much that this is one record I'm bashful about beating," he had said in the days leading up to the record. "Something doesn't seem to be right about it."

There would be no stopping his march to history. During a power play with just over five minutes remaining in the second period, Gretzky took a cross-ice pass from Marty McSorley and, with Canucks goalie Kirk McLean out of the play, redirected the puck into the net for number 802. The L.A. Forum went into a frenzy as Gretzky was engulfed by his teammates, who leapt *en masse* from the Kings bench to celebrate.

The game was stopped for a brief ceremony during which NHL commissioner Gary Bettman presented Gretzky with a book containing a score sheet from every game in which he had scored.

Gretzky accomplished the feat in just 1117 games. Howe scored his 801 in 1767. Both Howe and Gretzky also played professionally in the World Hockey Association. When combining numbers from both leagues, Gretzky finished his career with 1072 goals, just one more than Howe.

JAMES**DUTHIE**

REMEMBERS

❝ Here is a guy who admired Gordie Howe so much, it was a thrill for him to break the record and to be No. 1, but also to get it done so people would stop talking about it. I think that Wayne is very much into that. He, as much as he adored scoring goals and breaking records, didn't love the attention all that much. ❞

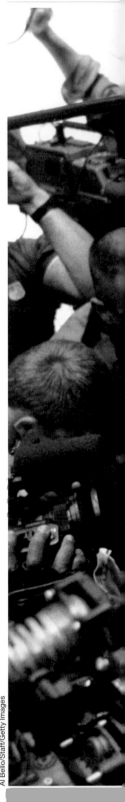

Al Bello/Staff/Getty Images

Wayne Gretzky surpassed his boyhood idol Gordie Howe to become the NHL's all-time scoring leader, a record "The Great One" is likely to hold for a long time.

1994

LUI TO THE RESCUE

Grey Cup Stays in Canada

Lui Passaglia's field goal with no time left on the clock gave B.C. a dramatic Grey Cup win over Baltimore to keep the venerable trophy on Canadian soil.

John Sokolowski

CHRIS CUTHBERT

REMEMBERS

❝ I broke my own protocol as a broadcaster and jumped in the air after the Lui Passaglia field goal. I ran down to the field to conduct post-game interviews with the Canadian players and Vic Stevenson, the Canadian offensive lineman, was in tears. It was vindication for the Canadian players. They felt they deserved to stand next to the American players. ❞

The CFL's championship game has always held a special importance to Canadian football fans. But there was more on the line than usual at the 82nd Grey Cup at Vancouver's B.C. Place.

The CFL's expansion to the United States in the early 1990s meant that the venerable old trophy was at risk of going south. The B.C. Lions were suddenly playing not just for the pride of their team, but also the entire country. The Baltimore franchise, which joined the league in 1994 without a nickname thanks to a legal dispute with the NFL, was an immediate and surprising success. Taking second place in the East thanks to a 12–6 record, the team, now going by the name Baltimore CFLers and coached by CFL veteran Don Matthews, hammered the Toronto Argonauts 34–15 in the East Final to earn a spot in the Grey Cup. But thanks to an upset in the West, a 37–36 barnburner in which B.C. prevailed over

Calgary, their quest to become the first U.S team to win the Grey Cup would take place in the lions' den... against the Lions themselves. National pride was on the line.

Baltimore led at the half, but a touchdown plunge by B.C. backup quarterback Danny McManus, two B.C. field goals and another by Baltimore, knotted the score 23–23 late in the fourth quarter. With 1:02 remaining in the game, B.C kicker Lui Passaglia lined up to kick a 37-yarder that would pull the Lions ahead. The sound of 55,097 people groaning at the same time signalled his miss. Baltimore got the ball back but stumbled badly, leaving B.C. with good field position but short of time. Passaglia had one last crack at redemption. From 38 yards out, with no time left on the clock, he split the uprights for a 26–23 win that kept the Grey Cup in Canada . . . for one more year anyway.

FIGURE SKATER NANCY KERRIGAN IS ATTACKED BY FRIEND OF RIVAL

Kerrigan Regains Form in Time for an Olympic Showdown with Tonya Harding

The on-ice battle between two of America's top figure skaters turned into off-ice drama between Nancy Kerrigan, left, and rival Tonya Harding, right.

Pascal Rondeau/Allsport

Vincent Amalvy/AFP/Getty Images

ROD SMITH

REMEMBERS

" This was the biggest television soap opera you could find. It transcended all the boundaries for sports fans and non-sports fans alike. It was bizarre, it was trashy, it had a hero, it had a villain, and it had all the elements gossip-hounds loved. This one seemed like a classic soap opera in the world of sports. Juicy stuff. "

It was an incident that exemplified the very opposite of the Olympic spirit.

On January 6, defending figure skating champ Nancy Kerrigan was brutally attacked at Cobo Arena in Detroit during a practice session before the 1994 U.S. Figure Skating Championships. The assailant, Shane Stant, clubbed her in the knee with a sledgehammer, eliminating her from the competition and from possible qualification for a spot in the upcoming Olympic Winter Games in Lillehammer, Norway.

It was later revealed that Stant had been hired by Jeff Gillooly, the ex-husband of one of Kerrigan's skating rivals, Tonya Harding. Harding went on to win the U.S. women's title and earn a spot on the Olympic team. As the story was revealed, the U.S. Olympic Committee launched proceedings to have Harding removed from the team but backed off when Harding threatened a lawsuit. The committee also granted Kerrigan a spot on the team, setting the stage for high drama in Lillehammer. The February 23rd broadcast of the women's short program drew 45.69 million viewers, the sixth-largest television audience in U.S. history.

Ultimately, the showdown was a letdown as Kerrigan skated wonderfully and finished with a silver medal while a disgraced Harding faded to eighth. She eventually pled guilty to hindering the investigation into the attack on Kerrigan and was sentenced to three years probation and 500 hours of community service and a large fine. Harding's notoriety — she was featured on the covers of *Time* and *Newsweek* — did not serve her well in the skating world, where she was shunned by the lucrative pro circuit.

1994

MARK MESSIER CARRIES NEW YORK RANGERS AND THEN CUP

Rangers Capture Their First Championship in 54 Years With a Game 7 Win Over Vancouver Canucks

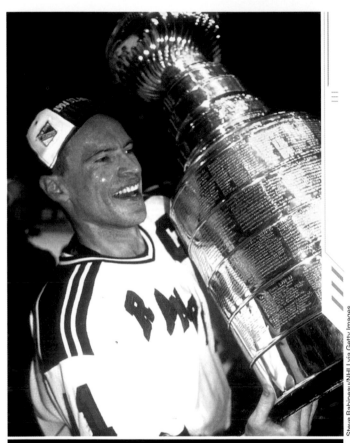

Mark Messier helped end a Stanley Cup drought of more than half-a-century in New York.

Steve Babineau/NHLI via Getty Images

It was hockey's longest drought. The New York Rangers, a stalwart franchise from the Original Six era, had played 54 seasons since their last Stanley Cup win in 1940. But coming into the playoffs following the 1993–94 season, things were looking up. The Rangers were the best team in hockey, amassing an impressive 112 points. And with the still-productive remnants of the Edmonton Oilers dynasty now in their lineup — including captain Mark Messier, Glenn Anderson, Craig MacTavish, Kevin Lowe and Esa Tikkanen — the team knew how to win the big games. Good thing.

After sweeping the New York Islanders and beating the Washington Capitals in five games, the Rangers faced a tough test against the New Jersey Devils in round three, falling behind the Devils 3–2 in games. With confidence in the Rangers seeming to slip among the fans and perhaps among his teammates, captain Mark Messier put the team on his shoulders, publicly guaranteeing a win in Game 6. Under enormous pressure, Messier backed up his prediction by scoring a third-period hat trick to lead the Rangers to a 4–2 win before going on to take the series in seven games.

The Stanley Cup final would pit the Rangers, and a now-expectant fan base, against the seventh seed from the Western Conference, the upstart Vancouver Canucks, who had upset the Calgary Flames, Dallas Stars and Toronto Maple Leafs on their unlikely Cup run. Led by the "Russian Rocket," Pavel Bure, and heart-and-soul captain Trevor Linden, the Canucks had confidence and a knack for scoring the big goal at the right time.

If the Rangers expected an easy series, that was dashed after the Canucks took Game 1, in New York, in overtime. The Rangers bounced back with three consecutive wins and came home for Game 5 with a chance to clinch. But the parade that the city had already planned would have to wait, as Vancouver beat the Rangers 6–3. Back in Vancouver, the Canucks marched on with a 4–1 win, knotting the series at three.

Game 7 in New York was electric, with the Madison Square Garden faithful anticipating the Cup. The Rangers took a two-goal lead twice, but both times Canuck captain Linden scored to pull his team back to within one — including a short-handed effort in the second period. Ultimately, it was Messier's goal late in the middle frame that proved to be the winner, even though the Canucks would press until the dying seconds, including three faceoffs in the New York zone over the final 38 seconds. New York goalie Mike Richter would hold his ground for a 3–2 win, and the Rangers would hold the Cup high for the first time in more than five decades.

It was widely agreed that the win was great exposure for hockey in the huge New York market, where the four daily newspapers ran a combined total of 42 pages of stories and photos. The parade three days later was attended by an estimated 1.5 million fans and led by new mayor Rudolph Giuliani, who had been at Game 7. He called Messier "Mr. June," a moniker that hearkened back to another New York sports icon, Yankees' Reggie Jackson, who was known as "Mr. October" for his clutch hitting.

Robert Laberge/Allsport

The Rangers were the best team in hockey during the 1993-94 season, largely due to the famous leadership of their captain.

RAY**FERRARO**

REMEMBERS

" The Rangers, the fans, the organization were so starved for success, because they literally had had very little opportunity to win the Cup for many years. In '94 they had a fantastic team, and they made some deals at the deadline that really made them a team that many felt could win that year. After escaping the New Jersey series where they had to go into Jersey and win the famous Messier guarantee game, they get to the Stanley Cup final. It turned out to be an incredible series and an unbelievable Game 7. The worst part about the Rangers winning was that fabulous 1940 chant was gone. The attention that it brought to our sport in the United States was unbelievable.

Glenn Healy's a good friend of mine. He was backup goaltender for the Rangers. And I remember seeing him on one of the cars in the parade and it was just unbelievable, this outpouring of pent up emotion that the fans had. Those players will be remembered in New York forever. "

1995

JOHN DALY UNLIKELY BRITISH OPEN CHAMP

Daly Hoists Claret Jug After Playoff Forced by Costantino Rocca's Impossible Putt

Costantino Rocca turned in one of the gutsiest performances in British Open history . . .

Andrew Redington/Allsport

Rarely has a major championship come down to a contest between two more unlikely characters. Twenty-nine-year-old American John Daly, twice suspended from the PGA Tour, was golf's "bad boy" of the tour. He had also played poorly all season and finished last twice in his first three British Open starts. But that week at the Royal and Ancient Golf Club of St. Andrews, the renowned long-ball hitter somehow found his game. Able to drive six of the par fours and hit short irons into the par fives, and displaying a deft touch on and around the tricky greens, Daly began the final round in third place,

just four strokes behind third-round leader Michael Campbell. By the time he tapped in at the 18th for a final-round 71, he found himself with the clubhouse lead and just one group left to finish.

His remaining challenger, in the final group with Campbell, was Italian Costantino Rocca, a good-natured late bloomer who had become a steady competitor on the European Tour. Needing a birdie on the par-four 18th to tie Daly, Rocca smashed a drive up the left side of the fairway, almost reaching the green. Needing to get up and down for the birdie, he then mishit his pitch, leaving him still off the green 60 feet from the cup in an undulation known on the legendary course as the Valley of Sin. Standing behind the green with his wife, his agent and his caddy, Daly had every reason to believe he had won and even allowed himself a hug and a smile with his wife.

Rocca putted the ball, and, incredibly, it raced toward the hole and dove in for birdie. The stunned crowd erupted as the Italian golfer, overcome with emotion, fell to the ground, joyfully beating his hands into the turf. Daly's face sunk in disbelief.

Instead of crumbling, Daly steeled himself and continued his stellar play in the four-hole playoff to decide the tournament. After a good par at the first, he rolled in a 35-foot birdie on number two to grab a two-shot lead. By the time Rocca putted out on the 17th, after a run-in with the Road Bunker, he was marking seven on his card, and Daly needed only a routine par on the 18th to win the playoff by four and hoist the Claret Jug.

It was Daly's second major title after his 1991 PGA Championship. With the win, he joined an elite group of golfers in the post–Second World War era — at the time including only Jack Nicklaus, Johnny Miller and Tom Watson — to win two majors before the age of 30.

Jean-Loup Gautreau/AFP/Getty Images

. . . but it wasn't enough to stop John Daly from kissing the Claret Jug.

BOB**WEEKS**

REMEMBERS

❝ Coming into the Open Championship, I don't think anybody suspected that Daly would have the kind of game that would win a British Open, or be playing well enough at that time to win. But he got in and posted the lowest score on the board, and the only person who could beat him was Costantino Rocca. Rocca got to that last hole and made an impossible shot from a place called The Valley of Sin that nobody ever makes. I think the poignant moment for me was, there was Daly sort of not quite ready yet to celebrate but looking over. And when he saw that putt go in, you could read his lips, and he said, 'Oh my God, he made it.' And at that point I think you know he was the most stunned person of all and you could see Rocca on his knees kind of thanking the heavens that this putt had gone in. Of course they went into a playoff and Daly won fairly handily. And here was John Daly, sort of the wild thing, the guy from Arkansas, this kind of self-confessed red neck, holding the oldest trophy in professional golf. It was one of the more remarkable days that we had seen in golf for a long time. ❞

CAL RIPKEN PASSES LOU GEHRIG

Baltimore Orioles Shortstop Becomes New "Iron Man"

From the beginning of the 1995 season, Cal Ripken Jr.'s 15th in the majors, the entire baseball world was waiting for a September 6th game between the Baltimore Orioles and the California Angels, when Ripken would pass — if all went well — legend Lou Gehrig's record for consecutive games played. It was an incredible feat. Gehrig, the Hall of Famer New York Yankees first baseman, known as "the Iron Horse," was one of baseball's most admired stars, who had been forced from the game by illness. Before Ripken, no player had come within 800 games of Gehrig's mark. But the Orioles' perennial all-star's rare combination of durability and dedication, combined with an uncompromising work ethic, had brought him to the brink of the "untouchable" record. It was all the more impressive considering he played shortstop, one of the busiest positions on the diamond.

The capacity crowd at Camden Yards that night included both U.S. President Bill Clinton and Vice-President Al Gore. As the Angels' half of the fifth inning ended and the game became official, the large banners displaying Ripken's streak beyond the right-field wall turned from 2130 to 2131. The entire crowd, including the Angels team and the umpires working the game, erupted in an ovation that lasted for 22 minutes. Pushed out of the dugout and onto the field by teammates, the normally restrained Ripken ran a lap around the stadium, shaking hands and high-fiving fans. Broadcaster ESPN did not cut to commercial during the entire ovation. It was one of the network's all-time highest-rated broadcasts.

Ripken's march to the record was celebrated throughout the season by Major League Baseball. It provided a positive story for the league amid dropping attendance and general backlash following the players strike of 1994. Ripken's streak, which began on May 30, 1982, finally ended before the Orioles' final home game of the 1998 season, when Ripken would take himself out of the lineup after 2632 consecutive games played.

Brian Bahr/AFP/Getty Images

Cal Ripken's consecutive-games record pursuit was the good-news story of baseball in 1995.

BUCK MARTINEZ

REMEMBERS

❝The streak actually began against Toronto in 1982. We had heard about this young talent who was coming up with Baltimore and was going to be the next Brooks Robinson at third. We saw him come in a game on May 30th and make the switch to shortstop and all of a sudden he was now a shortstop. Little did we know that night was the start of a streak that would lead to Lou Gehrig's record being broken. I was a part of that broadcast. The thing about Cal was that he was a phenomenal athlete with a lot of great skills who kept himself in great shape. He took a lot of pride in keeping himself healthy and keeping himself ready to play. He told me many times, "You want to know about the streak? I'm a baseball player. I'm supposed to play baseball games. My team counts on me to play and there is no reason why I shouldn't play." He was just all about playing the game he was supposed to because he was a baseball player. ❞

O.J. SIMPSON FOUND NOT GUILTY

Simpson's Murder Trial and Verdict Become Must-See TV for Millions

The O.J. Simpson murder trial began on January 25, 1995, and for eight months captivated the public like no other legal event in history. Simpson had pleaded not guilty in the brutal murders of his ex-wife, Nicole Brown Simpson, and her acquaintance Ronald Goldman. The trial pitted the Los Angeles County prosecutor's office, led by Marcia Clark and Christopher Darden, against Simpson's own bevy of defence lawyers, dubbed the "Dream Team," which included, among others, F. Lee Bailey, Johnnie Cochran and Robert Shapiro.

While the prosecution focused on DNA evidence and Simpson's violent relationship with his ex-wife, the defence attempted to discredit the Los Angeles Police Department and the reliability of the evidence, insinuating that a form of institutional racism was at work. The most dramatic moment came when Simpson was asked to try on a pair of bloody gloves, one of which was found at the crime scene, the other at Simpson's home. At trial, they appeared not to fit. As the trial drew to a close, the public was largely divided along racial lines, and there were fears that a guilty verdict could result in rioting similar to what had followed the Rodney King affair. When the jury returned after less than four hours of deliberation with a verdict of

Fred Goldman and Kim Goldman, Ronald Goldman's father and sister, at the murder trial.

Ethan Miller/Getty Images

not guilty, there was only cheering from assembled crowds and disbelief from the victims' families. The reading of the verdict was watched by an estimated 150 million Americans — and countless others around the world.

Simpson, who had been held in custody for 473 days, was ordered immediately released, and the longest jury trial in California history came to an end.

The trial was preceded by one of the strangest spectacles in television history, also involving Simpson. On June 17, 1994, millions of people were glued to their sets as a white Ford Bronco containing the former football star led a fleet of Los Angeles Police Department squad cars on a low-speed freeway chase. It was five days after the bodies of Nicole Brown Simpson and Ronald Goldman had been discovered murdered at Goldman's condominium. Initial investigations led police to believe O.J. was a prime suspect. After he failed to turn himself in, the chase was on, eventually ending at Simpson's home where he surrendered to authorities.

Al Bello/Allsport

Shapiro was a member of O.J. Simpson's "Dream Team" of lawyers.

DARREN DUTCHYSHEN

REMEMBERS

❝ I thought it was as cut and dried a case as you could possibly have. I thought the evidence was overwhelming. I thought O.J. was going to be found guilty. When they said "not guilty," I was stunned. I could not believe it and I still can't believe it to this day. It just seemed so contradictory to the evidence and everything we had heard. I watched a lot of the trial. I was sucked in because it was O.J. But that was one moment that I will remember for the rest of my life. ❞

Team Canada was virtually unstoppable at the 1995 World Junior Championships held in Red Deer, AB, in 1995, going undefeated on the way to the country's third gold in a row, during a run of five consecutive titles.

Doug MacLellan/Hockey Hall of Fame

PATRICK ROY'S LAST GAME AS A HAB

Saint Patrick Demands a Trade after Humiliation at Hands of Detroit Red Wings

Patrick Roy's career with the Habs was the stuff of legend, but his departure was sudden and shocking.

Rick Stewart/Allsport

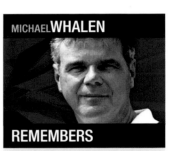

MICHAEL WHALEN

REMEMBERS

&6 I watched that game on TV, so I saw what everybody else saw, and I didn't get a sense then that Patrick wanted out of the Canadiens. But certainly that was common knowledge after the game and the first thing in the morning I got a phonecall telling me to head down to the Forum. There was a horrendous storm that day. I arrived and there was a smattering of people there, but bit by bit more people started showing up, and soon we all had a sense that a trade was coming. It was late in the afternoon when Réjean Houle finally came down to announce Patrick had been traded to the Colorado Avalanche. And from there the whole thing snowballed into a media frenzy, and it was not just sports media covering it, it was all the news stations and national media as well. Before he left, Patrick held his own press conference up in Laval, which was a little bizarre for a player to do. But you should have seen the people there. I don't think people realized the power Patrick had until then. When he left it was the end of an era in Montreal. And the Canadiens haven't come close to winning since. 99

It was an unfortunate end to a stellar career in Montreal. During a Saturday-night game in early December, Patrick Roy — Saint Patrick to the legions of Habs faithful who watched him brilliantly backstop the team to two Stanley Cups — was having perhaps his worst night ever between the pipes. With the Montreal defence overmatched and Roy unable to stem the tide, the ultra-potent Detroit Red Wings offence beat him nine times in just 31 minutes. Montreal fans had begun to offer mock cheers when he did make a save, to which Roy raised his arms above his head in mock celebration. It wasn't pretty.

Finally — and, to many hockey minds, including Roy's, too late — he was pulled from the game by head coach Mario Tremblay. Roy and Tremblay were rumoured to have had a poor relationship before the incident, but for the famously feisty goalie, this was too much. His pride shattered, an angry and a humiliated Roy left the ice and deposited his stick, gloves and mask in the tunnel before storming toward his spot near the end of the players bench. A couple of steps past Tremblay, Roy stopped, turned and delivered a simple, pointed message to Canadiens president Ronald Corey sitting nearby: "It's my last game in Montreal."

Unable to smooth things over or placate Roy, general manager Réjean Houle dealt his goalie to Colorado four days later in a blockbuster trade that also saw Mike Keane join the Avalanche and goaltender Jocelyn Thibault and forwards Andrei Kovalenko and Martin Rucinsky come to Montreal.

Sadly for Habs fans, the trade did more for Colorado, who went on to win the Stanley Cup later that spring and would win again in 2001 with Roy in the net. Roy's infamous last game in Montreal ended 12–1 Detroit. It was the Canadiens' worst home loss in franchise history.

1996

GREY CUP CLASSIC HIGHLIGHTED BY MIRACLE CATCH

Edmonton's Eddie Brown Makes Shoestring Catch and Scampers to 64-Yard Touchdown

The 1996 Grey Cup was a Canadian football classic. The -10° C temperature and steady snowfall throughout the game provided the backdrop for two red-hot quarterbacks — Danny McManus of the Edmonton Eskimos and Doug Flutie of the Toronto Argonauts — to throw for a combined 715 yards in an offensive gem that was pure CFL magic.

Despite the weather, the crowd of 38,595 at Hamilton's Ivor Wynne Stadium witnessed one of the better-played league finales in history, with no fumbles and just six penalties — and one of the greatest plays in Grey Cup history. Nearing the end of the first quarter, McManus hit wide receiver Eddie Brown along the sideline. The ball initially struck Brown in the thigh and fell to his foot, where he literally made a shoestring catch before romping 64 yards for a touchdown and a 9–0 Eskimo lead. It left many wondering whether Toronto's day was done.

Flutie would answer, emphatically, in the second quarter, putting up a league-record 27 points — of a combined 41 by both teams — to have Toronto storm back and take a 27–23 halftime lead. That quarter also saw two incredible returns for touchdowns. The first, an 80-yard punt return by the Argos' Jimmy Cunningham, was answered less than 10 minutes later by the Eskimos' Henry "Gizmo" Williams as he returned a kickoff 91 yards for a score.

The shootout continued in the second half, but Edmonton could never regain the lead. The Eskimos scored with nine seconds left, to cut the lead to six but failed to recover the ensuing onside kick, and Toronto held on for a 43–37 victory.

In retrospect, it was the kickers who had decided the game. Toronto's Mike Vanderjagt converted five of five field-goal attempts while Edmonton's Sean Fleming went zero for three. For his efforts, Vanderjagt was named Canadian Player of the Game. Flutie was named Grey Cup MVP, the second of three such awards he would collect over his Hall of Fame career.

JOCK CLIMIE

REMEMBERS

❝ It was one of those sports moments when you knew something just happened but it didn't look right. It all happened so fast you say to yourself, "I couldn't have seen what I just saw." You're wondering if the ref's going to blow the whistle, and it's not until they play it back that you realize it went off his hand, off a leg, and then off a foot and then back into his hand. There were three aspects to it: the catch itself, which, if it was made in a pre-season game by a rookie no one would have ever thought of it again, even though people at that game still would have been amazed by it. The second aspect was that it was in the snow. It was a picturesque scene with flurries coming down and he makes this miraculous catch with snow flying everywhere. The third aspect, of course, was that it was the biggest game of the year. Despite the fact that there's a luck component to it, it still takes a tremendous amount of skill, hand-eye coordination, and talent to execute a play like that, even when the ball bounces your way. I wouldn't be surprised if we don't see it again — in our lifetime anyway. ❞

Eddie Brown will forever be remembered for his amazing Grey Cup catch in the snow.

DONOVAN BAILEY RACES TO 100-METRE GOLD

Canadian Sprinter Erases Memories of Ben Johnson Scandal

As the 1996 Olympic Summer Games in Atlanta approached, many Canadians were still living with the spectre of the Ben Johnson steroid scandal. Johnson had electrified the country by capturing Olympic gold in the 100 metres in Seoul in 1988 only to bring national shame in forfeiting the medal when he tested positive for steroid use following the race.

If the nation needed redemption, it was in Donovan Bailey's hands to provide it. Bailey had shot onto the international athletics scene with gold medals in the 100 metres and the 4 x 100-metre relay at the 1995 World Championships in Gothenburg, Sweden. Like Johnson, Bailey was a Jamaican-born Canadian, but he prided himself on being a "clean" runner who never touched performance-enhancing drugs. And he was peaking at exactly the right time.

In the racing style that had become his trademark, Bailey started relatively slowly in the gold-medal final — which was delayed by false starts and a distracting on-track protest from disqualified sprinter and 1992 gold medallist Linford Christie of England — before putting on a powerful mid-race surge to snatch victory in an Olympic- and world-record time of 9.84 seconds. Immediately after crossing the finish line, Bailey was wide-eyed and open-mouthed in celebration as he galloped around the track in victory. It was the signature image of the 1996 Summer Games, putting to rest the painful memories of the Johnson scandal. Canada had a new hero and his name was Donovan Bailey.

Bailey would earn double gold in Atlanta, anchoring the men's 4 x 100-metre relay team. He was just the second sprinter to hold all major 100-metre titles concurrently (world champion, Olympic champion and world record); American Carl Lewis was the first.

Bongarts/Getty Images

The great Donovan Bailey dominated on the track, on American soil, at the 1996 Olympic Summer Games in Atlanta.

BRIAN**WILLIAMS**

REMEMBERS

❝ Winning the men's 4 x 100 relay is one of the greatest accomplishments in Summer Olympics history for Canada. The United States had dominated this event for the better part of a century, and to have the Canadians beat them, on their own soil, was an incredible achievement. I don't think there was anyone who didn't feel great pride, especially with such a well-spoken, articulate group of young men representing your country with such class on the world stage, in such a marquee event. ❞

FORUM FAITHFUL HONOUR THEIR "ROCKET"

Habs Legend Receives Six-Minute Ovation at Closing of Hockey Shrine

Robert Laberge/Getty Images

In a long list of greats, Montreal's Maurice "The Rocket" Richard was perhaps the greatest.

Even for a career filled with highlights and honours, it was an exceptional tribute. On March 11, the Montreal Canadiens played for the final time at the legendary Montreal Forum. Following the game, a 4–1 win over the Dallas Stars, the team held a closing ceremony and invited many former Habs onto the Forum ice for a final farewell and a passing of the torch. The list of honorees included some of the greatest players in the history of the game. Jean Béliveau, Doug Harvey, Guy Lafleur, Larry Robinson, Bernie Geoffrion and Bob Gainey, among others, all took their place, each receiving a warm tribute from the crowd.

Maurice Richard, the greatest star in Canadiens history, was introduced last. What followed was the longest standing ovation in Montreal history. For more than six minutes, the capacity crowd stood and applauded and chanted his name. As the ovation continued, the normally restrained "Rocket" was moved to tears, as was his wife watching in the stands. He waved in acknowledgment and mouthed the words "Thank you" to the fans. For the final few minutes, Richard — whose brother Henri was also on the red carpet not far away — closed his eyes. He would later say that the sound of the chanting crowd brought him back to his younger days as a player.

Recalling the evening, Hockey Hall of Fame broadcaster Dick Irvin Jr., whose father coached the "Rocket" in his heyday, remembered the ovation with astonishment. "What other athlete, any place, any time, would get that kind of ovation from that kind of an audience?" Irvin rhetorically asked *Maclean's* magazine. "It showed what he meant to Quebec and to Montreal. And it wasn't just francophones — he was a hero to anglophones too."

A few days later, the Habs would move into their new home, the Molson Centre, a few blocks away. And it was there in 2000 that some 115,000 people again paid tribute to the "Rocket" — this time silently — as they filed past his coffin to offer their last respects. He died on May 27 of that year. It was one of the biggest outpourings of emotion the city had ever seen.

GREG NORMAN'S MASTERS-FUL COLLAPSE

Norman Starts Final Round at Augusta With Six-Shot Lead But Falls Apart

Greg Norman collapses after missing a shot.

Stephen Munday/Allsport

Nick Faldo was the beneficiary of the Norman non-conquest.

Stephen Munday/Allsport

The final round of the 1996 Masters was supposed to be one of the greatest in Greg Norman's life, a crowning achievement in his prestigious golfing career. Instead, it was one of the most unforgettable days in professional golf history, for the wrong reasons.

Beginning the round, Norman stood at a gaudy minus 13, thanks in large part to a course-record 63 on the opening day, and held a seemingly invincible six-shot lead over Nick Faldo. Having had the coveted green jacket dramatically torn from his grasp several times over his stellar career, this, it appeared, was Norman's turn to finally put it on.

As the players made the turn, however, Norman's masterful play during the first three rounds seemed a distant memory. With consecutive bogeys at nine, 10 and 11, his six-shot lead had vanished. On the next hole, the tricky par-three 12th, Norman plunked his tee shot into the water, leading to a double bogey. Faldo made another par. And in a stretch of four pars, the English golfer had picked up five strokes on Norman and grabbed a two-shot lead in the tournament.

The two players both went birdie, par, birdie, over 13, 14 and 15, with Norman narrowly missing a chip-in for an eagle on the 15th that would have pulled him back to within one. Still needing to make up two strokes in the final three holes, Norman hooked his tee shot on the par-three 16th into the water for another double bogey, handing Faldo a comfortable four-shot lead.

By now, Norman's swagger had been completely transformed into shock. Faldo birdied the 18th to put the final touches on his 67 for the low round of the weekend and his third Masters title. Norman finished with 78.

On the final green, Faldo hugged Norman. "I don't know what to say," he told Norman. "I just want to give you a hug. I feel horrible about what happened. I'm so sorry."

It was Norman's seventh and last second-place finish in a major (he won two British Opens). Hours after the collapse, Norman was somewhat philosophical about the round: "God, I'd love to be putting the green jacket on. But it's not the end of my life. I'm not going to fall off the face of the Earth because of what happened to me."

In the weeks following the event, he received hundreds of messages from people around the world expressing sympathy and recognizing the dignity he showed during the dramatic collapse.

1997

DETROIT ENDS CUP DROUGHT

Detroit Red Wings Sweep Philadelphia Flyers to Bring Stanley Home to Hockeytown

Rick Stewart/Allsport

|||

After the New York Rangers ended their Stanley Cup drought in 1994, the next longest remaining dry spell belonged to the Detroit Red Wings, who had not known NHL supremacy since the days of Gordie Howe and Ted Lindsay. By 1997, it had been 42 long years since fans in Hockeytown had celebrated a title. Coach Scotty Bowman's arrival for the 1993–94 season raised expectations, and the team did reach the Stanley Cup final in 1995 but lacked the ingredients necessary to go all the way. They were swept by the tougher, stronger and hungrier New Jersey Devils.

By the 1996–97 season, however, the transformation of the Red Wings under Bowman was nearly complete. Along with converting offensive-minded captain Steve Yzerman into one of the league's finest two-way players and assembling the devastating five-man unit of Sergei Fedorov, Igor Larionov, Slava Kozlov, Vyacheslav Fetisov and Vladimir Konstantinov, known as the "Russian Five," Bowman had weeded out players he felt were too soft for post-season success. The result was fewer regular-season wins — 24 fewer in 1996–97 than just a year earlier — but a grittier team to do battle in the playoffs.

The Red Wings took care of the St. Louis Blues and Anaheim Mighty Ducks in the first two rounds to reach their third consecutive Western Conference final. Avenging their loss from a year before, Detroit won a punishing six-game series over the defending Stanley Cup champion Colorado Avalanche to reach the final against the Philadelphia Flyers.

With Yzerman providing inspirational leadership, Fedorov and Brendan Shanahan leading the scoring punch and goaltender Mike Vernon playing some of the finest hockey of his career, the Wings made it all seem a formality, controlling the series from the start and sweeping the Flyers away in four games to the mad delight of their dedicated fans. Detroit held the Flyers to just six goals all series, and just one from captain Eric Lindros.

Vernon was awarded the Conn Smythe Trophy as playoff MVP. Amazingly, through the playoffs, the Red Wings were 16–0 when any of the "Russian Five" scored a point and 0–4 when they didn't. It was Bowman's seventh

The Detroit Red Wings started to reclaim the deed to Hockeytown with their first
Stanley Cup win in more than four decades.

Stanley Cup. During the celebration following Game 4 in Detroit, he donned his skates and went on the ice to hoist the Cup and congratulate his players.

The celebrations in Detroit were sadly and suddenly ended six days after the victory when a limousine carrying Konstantinov, Fetisov and team masseur Sergei Mnatsakanov hit a tree. While Fetisov made a full recovery, Konstantinov had severe head injuries and lost most of his motor skills. Although his hockey career was over, he did regain the ability to walk with the aid of a walker.

DARREN**DREGER**

REMEMBERS

❝ What I really remember about that year was Mike Vernon. He was vilified in '95 when they were swept by the New Jersey Devils and boy, talk about vindication. You can go down the list of great players they had, and it's pretty obvious that the '97 final was the Wings' coming-out party. They snapped a 42-year Stanley Cup drought, and with the coaching, the depth and the goaltending they had, you got a sense that going forward, they could be the next dynasty. ❞

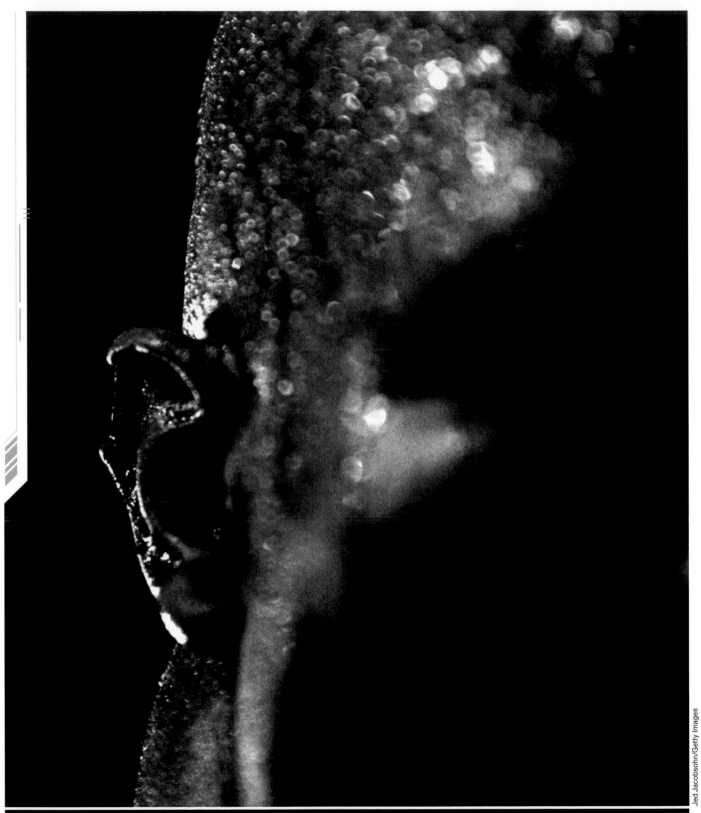

Mike Tyson chomped down on both of Evander Holyfield's ears in one of the most bizarre spectacles boxing has ever witnessed.

Jed Jacobsohn/Getty Images

EVANDER HOLYFIELD SURVIVES HEAVYWEIGHT BITER MIKE TYSON

A Shocked Holyfield Endures Double-Ear Biting in Bizarre Vegas Bout

Holyfield–Tyson II. The Sound and the Fury. However it was billed at the time, the rematch between Evander Holyfield and Mike Tyson may be best remembered to the world at large as the "Bite Fight."

Seven months earlier, in the fighters' first bout, Holyfield, a 25–1 underdog when betting opened, had shocked the world, knocking "Iron Mike" down, for just the second time in his career, in the sixth round and winning a technical knockout in the 11th round. For boxing fans starved for drama in the heavyweight division, either watching pay-per-view or in attendance at the MGM Grand Garden Arena in Las Vegas, the $100 million rematch was a dream bout and an enormous payday for both fighters — $30 million for Tyson and $35 million for Holyfield.

As the fight began, it looked like Holyfield would have his way again. Constantly charging forward and landing hooks and jabs, he owned the first two rounds, forcing Tyson to retreat and preventing him from using his jab or his power. Early in the second round, Holyfield inadvertently leaned in and head-butted Tyson, opening a large cut above his right eye. To the disgust of Tyson and his corner, referee Mills Lane did not deduct a point for the incident.

Clearly frustrated with the direction the fight was taking, Tyson rushed out of his corner for the third round, but Holyfield immediately noticed that he hadn't put in his mouthguard. Lane ordered Tyson back into the corner to put it in.

In the third, Tyson seemed to make some headway, but for some reason, late in the round, he chose to employ a barbaric tactic. Holding Holyfield in a clinch with just 40 seconds remaining, Tyson spit out his mouthguard, took Holyfield's right ear in his mouth and bit down hard, tearing off a large chunk. Holyfield turned around in pain and disbelief, blood streaming from his ear as Lane stepped in to halt the action.

After much discussion, Lane was ready to call the fight in favour of Holyfield, but when the fight doctor examined the partially earless fighter and determined he was okay, Lane elected to deduct two points from Tyson and let the bout continue. Little did he know that what was already a strange bout was about to get downright bizarre.

Just seconds after the fight restarted, Tyson attacked Holyfield again, this time biting off part of his left ear. As the round ended, those aware of what had happened were stunned. Holyfield stood in his corner, seemingly in shock. Lane stopped the fight seconds after the round ended, disqualifying Tyson. Mayhem ensued in the ring as boos rained down from the disgusted crowd and Tyson tried to get at Holyfield in his corner. Police and security were needed to calm the situation.

Ring announcer Jimmy Lennon Jr. then delivered these astonishing words to the boxing world: "Referee Mills Lane has disqualified Mike Tyson for biting Evander Holyfield on both of his ears."

Following the fight, Holyfield underwent surgery at the Valley Hospital Medical Center to repair the damage Tyson had done. Tyson was immediately suspended and lost his entire purse for the fight. He was later fined $3 million by the Nevada State Athletic Commision, which also revoked his licence to box. It would be 19 months before he would fight again.

RUSS ANBER

REMEMBERS

❝ I'll never forget Holyfield's reaction — the image of him grasping his ear and both his legs leaving the ground as he jumped up and down in pain while Tyson looked on with a look of almost disdain on his face. There have to be some serious underlying issues that would cause a fighter of this calibre, somebody who had been around as Mike Tyson had, to do something like that. ❞

CANADIAN JACQUES VILLENEUVE TAKES F1 TITLE

Quebec Race-Car Driver Follows in His Famous Father's Footsteps

F1 rivals Jacques Villeneuve and Michael Schumacher.

The final race of the 1997 F1 season in Jerez, Spain, amounted to a showdown for the driving title. Going into the race, two-time champion Michael Schumacher of the Ferrari team held a slim one-point lead over 26-year-old Canadian Jacques Villeneuve. Villeneuve, the son of the late Gilles Villeneuve, a six-time winner on the F1 circuit in the 1970s and 1980s, was a veteran of the CART IndyCar World Series, capturing rookie-of-the-year honours on the circuit in 1994 and winning the Indy 500 and the series title a year later. That experience would prove to be key to his title hopes.

As he had in the CART series, Villeneuve wasted no time in rising to the top in F1. Signed by Williams in 1996, Villeneuve won an F1-record four races in

his rookie season. With his teammate and defending champion Damon Hill gone to Arrows-Yamaha in 1997, Villeneuve became Williams' number-one driver, and he made the most of the opportunity, winning seven races and capturing 10 pole positions.

But he still trailed Schumacher as the two cars battled it out in Jerez. With Schumacher leading the race, during the 48th lap at a right corner known as Dry Sack, Villeneuve made a bold manoeuvre, moving quickly to the right to pass Schumacher on the inside. When the two cars were side by side, Schumacher turned suddenly to the right, ramming the wheel of his Ferrari into the side of Villeneuve's Williams-Renault. From his CART days, Villeneuve was accustomed to

The Canadian driver prevailed in the final race of the season to pass the German superstar in points and take the title.

bumping between vehicles, and despite damage to the left side of his car, he stayed in the race. Schumacher slid into a gravel runoff and was finished for the day.

Later in the race, Villeneuve allowed both McLaren drivers Mika Hakkinen and David Coulthard to pass him, knowing that to battle them might prevent him from finishing the race. When it was over, he finished third and captured the F1 title. Villeneuve, already a star in his native Quebec, would become one of the most beloved sports figures in the province.

Villeneuve is one of only three drivers to have won CART and F1 titles and the Indy 500. The others are Mario Andretti and Emerson Fittipaldi.

vicRAUTER

REMEMBERS

❝ In that last race, coming around the corner, Villeneuve dives inside and, sure enough, Schumacher actually drives into him. Literally drives into him. When he finally won the championship it was such a proud moment because it was something his father, who is still considered one of the best drivers ever, was never able to do. And he became the first Canadian world driving champion, so it was also as nationalistic a moment as any hockey game. ❞

1998

CANADA'S GOLD MEDAL HOPES SHOT DOWN

Wayne Gretzky Has Best Seat in the House to Watch Shootout

TV TOP 10 MOMENTS

1 Wayne Gretzky sits and watches as Canada loses to the Czechs in a shootout at the Olympic men's hockey semifinals.

2 St. Louis's Mark McGwire hits home run number 62 — breaking Roger Maris's record of 61 — with Chicago slugging rival Sammy Sosa watching on the field.

3 Michael Jordan steals the ball from Utah's Karl Malone and knocks down a jumper in the final seconds to give Chicago its sixth NBA title.

4 Dale Earnhardt celebrates finally winning the Daytona 500 — in his 20th attempt.

5 Canadian Sandra Schmirler's rink wins the first Olympic gold in curling with a win over Denmark.

6 Detroit's Steve Yzerman places the Stanley Cup on the lap of Vladimir Konstantinov, who suffered career-ending head injuries in a car accident one year earlier.

7 John Elway dives head first and is spun around like a helicopter to keep the winning drive alive as Denver beats Green Bay in the Super Bowl.

8 Ross Rebagliati wins Olympic snowboarding gold, becomes the first person stripped of a medal for having traces of marijuana in his system and then has it reinstated.

9 Mark O'Meara sinks an 18-foot birdie putt on the 18th hole to win the Masters.

10 Pittsburgh's Jerome Bettis calls "tails," but the referee says he hears "heads-tails" and awards Detroit possession to start overtime. Detroit wins the game.

The expectations for the 1998 Canadian Olympic men's hockey team were off the charts. With NHL players being allowed to participate for the first time, most Canadians viewed the Nagano 1998 Olympic Winter Games as Canada's chance to finally set right what they perceived as an Olympic-sized double standard. For years, the eligibility rules meant that the best Soviet players retained amateur status for international competitions while NHL players were ruled ineligible. As a result, Canada had not touched men's hockey gold since 1952. Adding to Canadians' hunger was the humbling loss at the hands of the United States in the inaugural World Cup of Hockey in 1996.

The super-team assembled by general manager Bob Clarke included names that spoke volumes on their own: Wayne Gretzky, Eric Lindros, Steve Yzerman, Joe Sakic, Ray Bourque, Patrick Roy and Martin Brodeur. Team Canada went undefeated in the round robin, outscoring their opponents 12–3 and recording a satisfying 4–1 win over the United States. An easy 4–1 win over Kazakhstan in the quarter-finals meant the Canadians would meet the Czech Republic in the semis.

Despite the presence of NHL offensive stars like Jaromir Jagr and Martin Straka, the Czechs' game was team defence and their best player unquestionably was Dominik Hasek, who already had three Vezina Trophies and one Hart Memorial Trophy and was midway through the 1997–98 NHL season in which he would win both again. He had already almost single-handedly sent the highly touted Americans home, stopping 38 shots in the Czechs' 4–1 quarter-finals win over the United States and had allowed a total of five goals in four games to that point in the tournament.

With Patrick Roy and Hasek squaring off in goal, Canadians back home,

Dominek Hasek dominated Canada in the infamous 1998 Olympic Winter Games shootout in Nagano.

Brian Bahr/Allsport

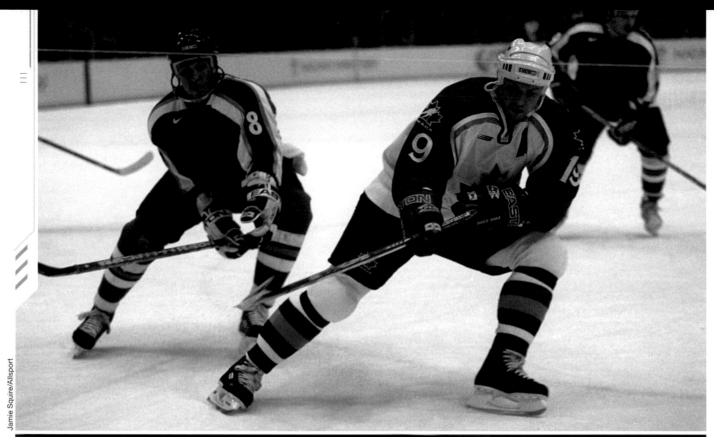

Team Canada left Japan medal-less, a crushing blow for a team that had its sights set on a first hockey gold for the country in nearly half a century.

waking in the early morning hours on Saturday, February 21 to watch the contest, knew they were in for a netminders' duel. Through two periods, both goalies had made a series of breathtaking saves to keep the score knotted at 0–0. The Czechs finally broke the tie with just over 10 minutes remaining in the third period. Off a faceoff win by Pavel Patera, defenceman Jiri Slegr skated in from the point and put a slapshot over Roy's right arm.

Things got tense for the Canadian team and all of Canada watching. With just over a minute left and Roy pulled from the net, Canada mounted a final offensive charge. Lindros entered the Czech zone and fed defenceman Al McInnis, who fired a shot on Hasek. Lindros then went behind the net to retrieve the rebound and fed it in front to Trevor Linden, who put the puck off Richard Smehlik's stick and over Hasek's glove for the tying goal. A 10-minute overtime was dominated by the Canadian team but settled nothing, and the game went to a shootout.

Each coach selected five shooters. Canadian coach Marc Crawford's list of Theoren Fleury, Bourque, Joe Nieuwendyk, Lindros and Brendan Shanahan was notable for the absence of the names Gretzky and Yzerman.

Following a Hasek stop on Fleury, Robert Reichel beat Roy with a perfect shot off the right post to give the Czechs a one-goal lead. And on bad ice, with Hasek in goal, it was all they would need. The closest Canada would come was when Lindros deked left and hit the right post. When Shanahan botched his deke attempt to the right, the Czech team poured from the bench in celebration, mauling Hasek as he raced from the net leaping into the air. A devastated Gretzky would remain on the bench long after his teammates left.

The team's fall was complete when it lost 3–2 to Finland in the bronze-medal game. For their part, the Czechs went on to defeat Russia 1–0 for the gold medal. In one of the great goaltending displays in history, Hasek had allowed only six goals in the six games of the tournament.

In the aftermath, much debate ensued about Crawford's decision not to use Gretzky and Yzerman in the shootout. Still more questions were raised about leaving Mark Messier off the team in the first place and putting the captaincy, and leadership duties, on a young Eric Lindros, his captain in Philadelphia.

BOB McKENZIE
REMEMBERS

❝ I understood the rationale that was given after the fact, that Gretzky was not great on breakaways, but I think most people felt that if there's a hockey game on the line and such high stakes as the Olympics, you want the best player in the game to have the game on his stick. I was as surprised as anybody that Gretzky didn't shoot. I think most Canadians wanted him on the ice with the puck on his stick and a chance to win it. It really boils down to eight simple words: win with your best, lose with your best. ❞

1998

SCHMIRLER THE CURLER WINS OLYMPIC GOLD

Canadian Women Rings Leader

Sandra Schmirler won the gold medal at the 1998 Winter Games in Nagano.

RAYTURNBULL

REMEMBERS

❝ The win had a huge positive effect for curling all around the world. It was an interesting week of competition. Sandra was an easy winner in the final game against Denmark, but had a very tight game in the semi-final against Kirsty Hay from Scotland. The game could have gone either way, but the Canadian champion once again came out on top. Sandra Schmirler's legend grew as she fought a long battle with cancer. When she died she left a huge hole in our sport, but her legacy lives on. ❞

As a young curler growing up in Biggar, Saskatchewan, Sandra Schmirler's dream was to "wear the green" of her provincial team. She never imagined that she would one day wear red and white for Canada in pursuit of Olympic gold.

If Schmirler and other curlers never dreamed of competing in the Olympic Games, it's probably because curling wasn't an Olympic event until it debuted at the Nagano 1998 Olympic Winter Games. Despite winning her third Canadian and world championships in 1997, a feat that remains unmatched, there was no free pass for Schmirler and her rinkmates Joan McCusker, Jan Betker, Marcia Gudereit, and alternate Anita Ford. They still had to compete against nine other teams in Olympic trials for the privilege of representing Canada at the upcoming Games. In November, only two months after the birth of her first child, Schmir-

ler skipped her rink to victory over an Alberta squad led by Shannon Kleibrink. Schmirler the Curler and her teammates were heading to Japan.

In Nagano, Schmirler and her crew eked out a 7–6 win over the United States, then came out on the wrong side of a 6–5, extra-end decision to Norway. Then they went on a roll, beating Japan, Denmark, Britain, Sweden and Germany to win the round-robin portion of the event with a 6–1 record. The Canadians advanced to the gold-medal final by beating Great Britain on Schmirler's final rock. The gold-medal match against Denmark was less dramatic but packed with emotion nonetheless. When it was all over, the first-ever winners of women's curling gold hugged one another while singing "O Canada!" The next day, Schmirler and crew were pictured on the front page of the New York Times under the headline "Gold Without Skates, Pads, or Spandex."

JORDAN'S JUMPER SEALS SIXTH BULLS TITLE

Chicago Bulls Superstar Carries Team to Victory in His Last Championship Game

Despite a 3–2 game lead over the Utah Jazz in the NBA finals, the Chicago Bulls' sixth title looked anything but secure. With less than a minute remaining in Game 6, Jazz point guard John Stockton had just hit a three-pointer to give his team an 86–83 lead. Never in their five previous NBA title runs had the Bulls been forced to seven games. And for Michael Jordan, in his final season with the Bulls, this was no time to start. Grabbing the ball off the inbound pass, he took it the length of the court and drove by Jazz guard Bryon Russell for a layup, cutting the lead to one.

The Jazz went to their bread and butter on the next possession, working the ball to Karl Malone in the post. The capacity crowd in Utah was prepared to explode if the "Mailman" could deliver just one more bucket to seal the victory. Jordan had other plans. He came from behind on Malone's right side and stripped the ball loose. Trailing by a point with just 18.9 seconds on the clock, the Bulls superstar opted not to call a time out, instead bringing the ball up court while surveying the Jazz defence. With Russell defending him closely, Jordan faked to his right before making a devastating crossover dribble back to his left. As Russell slipped down and out of the play, Jordan pulled up and drilled a 17-foot jump shot to put the Bulls up 87–86 with just 5.2 seconds to play.

The Jazz had one last chance, but when Stockton's three-pointer clanked off the rim, it was over. Jordan leapt into the air, and another celebration for the Bulls and their fans was underway.

It was the second year in a row the Bulls had defeated the Jazz in the finals. Jordan was named Finals MVP for the sixth time in Chicago's six championships. Coach Phil Jackson called it Jordan's best clutch performance ever to win a game. Jordan retired for the second time in his career on January 13, 1999. He would return once more, in 2001, before calling it quits for good after the 2002–03 season.

Jonathan Daniel/Allsport

Michael Jordan earned MVP honours in the NBA finals for the sixth time in his career.

MARK McGWIRE AND SAMMY SOSA GO TOE TO TOE IN HR PURSUIT

Cardinals and Cubs Sluggers Battle Down to the Wire in Pursuit of History

Mark McGwire won the famous, season-long home run derby to capture the single-season record.

Jed Jacobsohn/Getty Images Sport

As the 1998 baseball season got underway, the league was still feeling the effects of the 1994 strike. Many older fans still held on to their disdain, and younger fans showed less interest. An electrifying home-run race between sluggers Mark McGwire of the St. Louis Cardinals and Sammy Sosa of the Chicago Cubs would be instrumental in turning it all around.

As McGwire came into the year, expectations were already high for his chances to top the game's 27-year-old single-season home-run record. While other players, including Albert Belle and Ken Griffey, had threatened to get there after swatting 50 and 56 round-trippers in 1995 and 1997 respectively, "Big Mac" was the odds-on favourite to finally surpass the mark. And already with 27 homers at the end of May, they were safe odds. But he was not alone. In June, Sosa hit a record 20 home runs to increase his season total to 33 and tie Griffey, who was also in the mix. By the end of August, however, McGwire and Sosa were locked at 55, while Griffey's 47 left him well off the pace.

Through the summer and into September, the two enjoyed constant media attention. In stadiums, bars, homes and seemingly everywhere on the news, the home-run watch was on. Sosa's warm, candid personality was a welcome breath of fresh air for fans and even seemed to soften the more reserved McGwire.

McGwire got off to a fast start, reaching the 60 home-run mark on September 5. The stage was set for an incredible weekend of baseball, as the Cardinals welcomed Sosa and the Cubs to St. Louis for a three-game series. McGwire tied Roger Maris's long-standing mark on September 7 with a long blast off Cubs pitcher Mike Morgan. A day later, he drove a Steve Trachsel pitch just

Slammin' Sammy Sosa kept the competition close, matching McGwire blast for blast — almost.

over the left-field wall — a 341-foot dinger that was his shortest homer of the season — for record-breaking number 62. The Cubs infield applauded as he rounded the bases, and he was greeted at home plate by his son, who was working as the Cardinals bat boy. Sosa himself ran in from the outfield to congratulate McGwire, who literally lifted up his 200-pound rival with a hug as Cardinal fans went wild.

The two sluggers continued to battle and though a surge by Sosa put him in the lead with his 66th on September 25, McGwire settled the affair by hitting five in his final three games to end the season with 70.

Many thought McGwire's record would last for as many years as Maris's had, but it held only for three before Barry Bonds banged out 73 in 2001. In the years since the home-run frenzy, widespread allegations of steroid use by McGwire and Sosa have diminished the summer-long battle and the incredible offensive totals that resulted. During Congressional hearings into steroid use in baseball, McGwire gave inconclusive answers while Sosa seemed not to comprehend the questions he was being asked. McGwire finished his career with 583 after hitting 29 in his final season in 2001. Sosa hit 49 homers in 2002 for a 499 career total.

CHAPTER FOUR

1999–2003

CANADA'S SPORTS LEADER

By its 15th season, TSN was the very essence of a modern television network. When the world prepared to enter a new century, TSN was one step ahead of it, already firmly implanted in the digital age, with even more high-tech plans for the future.

In the meantime, TSN brought Canadians the triumphs and tragedies of the sports world better than ever before. The new 10 PM edition of SportsDesk, which soon became *SportsCentre*, was the highest-rated sports news program in the country. In 2003, TSN reached new heights with record ratings for the Canada-Russia gold-medal game at the IIHF World Junior Championship. And when Canadians rejoiced at the news of Vancouver winning its bid to host the 2010 Olympic Winter Games, they were watching TSN's live coverage.

As it prepared for its 20th anniversary, TSN became one of the first specialty channels to broadcast its signal in high definition. The future had arrived, and TSN was front and centre, offering coverage in ways people had never imagined, let alone seen.

Ezra Shaw/Getty Images

Mario the Magnificent helped secure Canada's first hockey gold in 50 years at the Salt Lake City 2002 Olympic Winter Games.

1999

TV TOP 10 MOMENTS

1 A controversial triple-overtime goal by Brett Hull, who has his skate in the crease, gives Dallas a Stanley Cup victory over Buffalo.

2 Wayne Gretzky retires with more than 50 NHL records, memorably skating around Madison Square Garden and waving to the New York Rangers faithful.

3 American soccer player Brandi Chastain takes off her jersey, revealing her sports bra, after scoring the winning goal on penalty kicks at the Women's World Cup

4 Needing only a double bogey on the par-four 18th hole to win the British Open, France's Jean Van de Velde takes a seven and loses in a playoff.

5 Mike Weir wins his first PGA event, capturing the Air Canada Championship in Vancouver. It's the first win by a Canadian on home soil since 1954.

6 Eighty-year-old baseball legend Ted Williams throws out the first pitch at the All-Star Game in San Francisco.

7 American road-racing cyclist Lance Armstrong wins his first Tour de France two years after battling cancer.

8 Justin Leonard sinks a 45-foot putt on the 17th hole to give the U.S. an emotional Ryder Cup victory over Europe in Brookline, Massachusetts

9 Stubby Clapp's routine fly ball to left field drops in and Canada beats the U.S. at the Pan American Games.

10 Canadian Olympic gold medallist Lennox Lewis, fighting as a Brit, wins a unanimous decision over Evander Holyfield to become the undisputed heavyweight champion of the world.

Ezra Shaw/Allsport

Wayne Gretzky calls an end to the most illustrious of careers in the same year he famously sported on the back of his jersey.

NO. 99 FOREVER

After a Career of Rewriting the NHL's Record Book, Wayne Gretzky Retires

The year 1999 turned out to be more than just the last one of the century. It was also the final year for No. 99, hockey great Wayne Gretzky, arguably Canada's finest athlete of the century.

Early in his 20th NHL season, his third with the New York Rangers, Gretzky gave little indication of his intention to say goodbye to hockey. But after being named MVP at the NHL All-Star Game, there was a sense that the end of an incredible career could be near. The first clue? After giving away the 19 vehicles he had won over the years, Gretzky kept the one awarded to him at the All-Star Game.

Soon after the regular season resumed, Gretzky hit yet another milestone. His 1071st goal tied him with Gordie Howe for most professional career goals. But the season was a trying one for both Gretzky and the Rangers. A scoring slump and neck injury combined to put off goal number 1072 for nearly two months. A month on the disabled list left Gretzky with a lot of time to ponder his future.

By the time Gretzky returned to the ice, the Rangers were out of the

Ezra Shaw/Getty Images

"The Great One" showed great emotion in his final game.

playoff hunt for the second straight season. Heading into the final week of the year, word started to spread that "The Great One" was pondering the unthinkable . . . retirement.

In the season's final days, Gretzky started giving clear indications that he was seriously considering hanging up his skates. Luckily for Canadian hockey fans, he had one final game in his home country, in the nation's capital. Anticipating that they might be witnessing the Great Gretzky's farewell tour, the fans in Ottawa spontaneously rose to their feet in salute.

The next day, Gretzky made it official at a press conference. "Sunday will be my last game," he said.

The tributes poured in, but there was still a final game to be played, against the Pittsburgh Penguins. The atmosphere was electric at Madison Square Garden, with former teammate Mark Messier among those turning up to send Gretzky off in style.

At the pre-game ceremony marking the occasion, NHL commissioner Gary Bettman announced that Gretzky's famous No. 99 would be retired leaguewide. It was a fitting tribute for the man who had won nine Hart Memorial Trophies as the NHL's MVP and who held, and still holds, just about every offensive record in hockey. There will never be another No. 99 skating in the NHL, just as there will never be another Wayne Gretzky.

TOUR DE FORCE

Two Years After Battling Cancer, Lance Armstrong Wins Cycling's Greatest Race

The Tour de France is one of sports' most gruelling events. Winning it is a momentous achievement, period. Winning it two years after being treated for cancer borders on the miraculous.

A former U.S. National Amateur champion, Lance Armstrong entered 1996 as the world's top-ranked cyclist. But something was wrong. Armstrong finished 12th in the road race at the Atlanta 1996 Summer Games, his second Olympics. He was forced to drop out of the Tour de France that year after becoming ill following the race's seventh stage. In October, Armstrong was diagnosed with an aggressive form of testicular cancer, one that spread to his lungs, stomach and brain. Doctors gave the 25-year-old less than a 50 percent chance of surviving.

After surgery and four rounds of chemotherapy, Armstrong was ready to make his professional comeback, one that got off to a rocky start. He quit in the middle of a Paris-Nice road race in early 1998, physically unable to go on. Many wondered whether it was the end for Armstrong, including Armstrong himself.

With an improvement in his health, he retreated to North Carolina for a rest, and it was there that he rediscovered his love for riding and the will to return to cycling's highest levels. In 1999, he had but one goal, to complete the Tour de France. He did much more.

Armstrong won the prologue time trial and four Tour stages, including the punishing first stage in the Alps. The final stage began with Armstrong wearing the famous yellow leader's jersey and ended with him wearing a smile as wide as Paris's Champs-Élysées. He finished the Tour seven minutes and 37 seconds ahead of second-place finisher Alex Zülle, dedicating his victory to cancer survivors everywhere.

Doug Pensinger/Allsport

Lance Armstrong dominated the Tour de France in the same year he beat cancer.

TOE-IN-THE-CREASE GOAL GIVES BRETT HULL AND DALLAS STARS STANLEY CUP

The Dallas Stars drank from Lord Stanley's Cup after defeating the Buffalo Sabres.

JAMES DUTHIE REMEMBERS

❝ I remember watching that game at home with my friends and everyone's initial reaction was "no goal." And when we saw the replay, we were only more certain. All year long, anything close to a little toe in the crease was reviewed. You could put together a video tape of so many goals waved off during the regular season for what seemed to be the same reason. I know the NHL said the rule allowed for Brett Hull to score in the crease. But it was rare for those kind of goals to count. I still go to Buffalo for the occasional game and Sabres fans have not forgotten about it. **❞**

Eddie Belfour and Stanley go for a skate.

After back-to-back championships, the Detroit Red Wings were once again favoured to sip from Lord Stanley's Cup. Instead, when 16 playoff contenders became a final two, the Stanley Cup final featured teams that had never won the Cup: the Dallas Stars and the Buffalo Sabres. The series was tight and hard fought, but the ending left a bad taste in some people's mouths.

To the chagrin of many, 1999 was the first year of a tough new application of the rule intended to protect NHL goaltenders from crease-crashing opposing forwards. If a team happened to score with one of its players, or even his little toe, in the forbidden zone, the goal wouldn't count. The rule was strictly applied throughout the regular season and into the playoffs.

With the final set, hockey fans got what they expected from the two hard-working and disciplined teams — low-scoring, intense hockey leading to triple overtime in Game 6 in Buffalo. With the Stars leading the series 3-2 and the score 1-1, Dallas sniper Brett Hull, positioned on the lip of Buffalo netminder Dominik Hasek's crease, knocked in a loose puck that set off a wild celebration. Video replays showed that Hull's skate was in the crease on the play. It was the type of goal that had been disallowed during the regular season. Pandemonium followed the goal, with the celebrating Stars swarming the ice and the Sabres trying to get the attention of the referees. NHL director of officiating Bryan Lewis later explained Hull was ruled to be in control of the puck and "allowed to shoot and score a goal even though the one foot (was) in the crease in advance of the puck." Sabre fans loudly disagreed.

1999

THE GREAT COLLAPSE

Jean Van de Velde Falls Apart on 72nd Hole of British Open

The 128th Open Championship, also known as the British Open, was held at the legendary Carnoustie Golf Links in Angus, Scotland. Golf's biggest names were on hand to challenge for the grand old game's oldest major. But by the time it was all over, it was a little-known French golfer whose name was on everyone's lips — and for all the wrong reasons. The beneficiary of his collapse, one of the greatest in sports history, was an equally obscure Scotsman.

Heading into the final round, Jean Van de Velde was at even par for the tournament, his near-flawless play providing him with a seemingly insurmountable five-

Atop the leaderboard on the final hole, the Frenchman imploded,

France's Jean Van de Velde's decision-making was all wet at the British Open.

stroke lead over Australian Craig Parry and the 1997 Open champion, American Justin Leonard.

Standing on the tee of the par-four 18th, his lead now down to three strokes, Van de Velde was still in an excellent position to win. All he needed was a double bogey to see his name inscribed on the legendary Claret Jug handed out to Open winners. But it was not to be. And with the first in what would be a series of bad decisions, Van de Velde pulled out a three-wood. His tee shot landed far to the right, not great, but not a total disaster either. Not yet, anyhow. Instead of counting his blessings and laying up with a short iron on his second shot, playing safely short of the famous water hazard Barry Burn, Van de Velde now pulled out a two-iron, figuring his lie was good enough for a shot at the green 230 yards away. That decision proved costly. His shot veered far off line, even farther right, bouncing backwards off the grandstand before bouncing yet again off the rocks on the banks of the burn and settling into some tall grass. The worst was not over. Van de Velde's third shot then landed in

David Cannon/Getty Images

Gerry Penny/AFP/Getty Images

making a triple-bogey seven to create a playoff — which he then lost.

Barry Burn. The crowd rumbled disapprovingly. And although he considered playing from the Burn, Van de Velde was forced to take a drop. Unbelievably, he was still in a position to win, needing a 63-yard pitch to the green and one putt. But the pitch ended up in a bunker. Van de Velde got his one putt, though, for a triple-bogey seven, which moved him into a tie with Leonard and Scotsman Paul Lawrie, who had started the day an incredible 10 strokes behind Van de Velde.

There was a four-hole playoff. But for Jean Van de Velde, the damage was done. His prematurely inscribed name had to be scratched off the Claret Jug. In its place was the name of Paul Lawrie, who recorded the biggest comeback in the history of golf's majors and became the first Scot to win on home turf since 1931.

As memorable as Lawrie's victory was, it is Van de Velde's great collapse that sports fans recall the most. Today, in any sport, blowing a tremendous lead through atrocious play, with victory close at hand, has come to be known as "pulling a Van de Velde."

Ross Kinnaird/Allsport

Scotsman Paul Lawrie might have kissed Van de Velde instead of the Claret Jug.

Led by goaltender Kim St. Pierre (below) and captain Thérèse Brisson (above) Team Canada beat the U.S. to capture gold at the 1999 Women's World Championship in Espoo, Finland.

Jed Jacobsohn/Getty Images Sport

After scoring the fifth penalty kick to ensure a U.S. victory over China in the 1999 Women's World Cup, midfielder Brandi Chastain peeled off her jersey.

2000

Steve Babineau/Hockey Hall of Fame

Marty McSorley's infamous stick ended his NHL career.

GROSS MISCONDUCT

Marty McSorley Found Guilty of On-Ice Assault of Donald Brashear

With one stick swing at the head of Vancouver Canucks tough guy Donald Brashear, Boston Bruins defenceman Marty McSorley put himself, the NHL and perhaps even the game of hockey on trial. The suspension he earned turned out to be the stiffest penalty the NHL has ever handed out, but to many, including the justice authorities in British Columbia, a different kind of penalty was called for.

The incident, which occurred with only three seconds left in the game and left Brashear unconscious on the ice, put the NHL and hockey violence in the spotlight once again. The scene was played and replayed on television countless times. The NHL predictably suspended McSorley, believed by many to be playing his final season even before the incident, for the season's remaining 23 games and the playoffs. But there were calls for punishment outside of hockey as well.

Two weeks later, B.C. prosecutors formally charged McSorley with one count of assault with a weapon. In September, McSorley entered a B.C. provincial courthouse for the trial that would determine his fate. The Crown portrayed McSorley's actions as going beyond the accepted norms of hockey. McSorley's defence was that he was only trying to challenge Brashear to fight, as they had earlier in the game, and that he'd simply missed Brashear's shoulder and accidentally struck his head. The judge didn't buy his version of events and found him guilty. His sentence, however, was an 18-month conditional discharge, meaning that he would not go to jail or have a criminal record.

One month later, NHL commissioner Gary Bettman announced that another year was being tacked on to the league's original suspension, a decision that effectively put an unfortunate end to Marty McSorley's 17-year NHL career.

attack on Donald Brashear led to a year-long suspension that effectively

JAMES DUTHIE

REMEMBERS

❝ This was probably the modern day defining moment of National Hockey League ugliness. Todd Bertuzzi's attack on Steve Moore a few years later was worse, mostly because Steve Moore broke his neck and Brashear wasn't that badly hurt. But this was a stick blow to the head. McSorley has always maintained that he was trying to poke him in the shoulder and trying to get him to fight again. But if you're a skilled hockey player, and Marty McSorley, for all his punching ability still had some skill, I just don't think you miss that badly.

As someone who covers hockey, for whom it is a livelihood but also a passion, it was a horrible time for the game. Some of the media in the U.S. only pays attention to hockey when something like this happens, so it's extremely frustrating. But at the same time, you have to acknowledge that it was worthy of that coverage because It was ugly and violent, and showed the dark side of the game. ❞

TURNING POINT

VINSANITY!

Toronto Raptor Vince Carter Takes NBA's All-Star Slam Dunk Contest

Toronto's Vince Carter led the NBA in highlights in 2000 — including taking the slam dunk title during All-Star Weekend — and led the Raptors to the playoffs for the first time ever.

Jed Jacobsohn/Allsport

Every NBA fan knew that Toronto Raptors guard Vince Carter was good, but at the All-Star Game in Oakland, California, he did things that humans were not supposed to do with a basketball, and a legend was born.

Vince Carter was already a league-wide sensation as the New Year began. His high-flying aerial act had captured the imagination of both fans and the media: images of him soaring through the air graced magazine covers, and the man some around the NBA were calling "Air Canada" was the leading vote-getter for the upcoming All-Star Game, garnering the second-highest vote total ever. But it was during the All-Star Weekend, specifically his electrifying performance in the slam dunk contest, that Carter exploded from fan favourite to phenom. His gravity-defying leaps and wizardry with the ball left mouths — including among his professional peers — agape. With an array of dunks, including a 360-degree reverse windmill and an elbow-in-the-rim dunk known as the honey dip or cookie jar, Carter blew the competition away. Walking away from his final dunk, a spectacular between-the-legs windmill, Carter looked into the courtside TV camera and mouthed the words that everyone was thinking: "It's over."

Carter was just getting started. After the All-Star break, he turned things up a notch. In the Raptors' first-ever appearance, shown nationally in the US on NBC, Carter had his way with the Phoenix Suns for a Raptors-record 51 points. In the weeks that followed, "Vinsanity" spread quickly. A series of dramatic individual performances, including a pair of buzzer beaters, helped send the Raptors to the franchise's first playoff appearance. "Air Canada" had taken flight, and all of Toronto was on board.

John Sokolowski © 2000

Kicker Lui Passaglia's two field goals and two singles helped the B.C. Lions defeat the Montreal Alouettes 28-26 in the thrilling 2000 Grey Cup. The two teams combined to score 32 points in the fourth quarter.

CANADA'S HIGHS AND LOWS DOWN UNDER

Inspirational Performances Salvage Disappointing Sydney 2000 Olympic Summer Games

Andy Lyons /Allsport

Canada's Simon Whitfield breaks the tape to win the inaugural — and incredibly exciting — men's triathlon.

Sydney, Australia promised to showcase an Olympic Games without parallel, and it delivered, with the famous Sydney Harbour providing a breathtaking backdrop to some unforgettable achievements.

For Canada, though, the 2000 Summer Games had more heartbreak than heroics. After seeing their medal total rise in each of the previous three Olympic Summer Games, culminating with a 22-medal haul in Atlanta, Team Canada fell off the podium. Flattened in boxing (0 medals), out of gas on the track (0 medals) and sinking in the pool (one bronze in swimming), Canadian athletes brought home a disappointing 14 medals. Some Canadian athletes, however, did deliver world-class performances. Victoria's Steve Nash, with MVP-like flair, showed heart and soul in leading Canada to an upset over hoops powerhouse Yugoslavia before bowing out to France in the quarter-finals.

And some Canadians showed they were prepared to rise to the top Down Under. Kingston, Ontario's Simon Whitfield surged from the pack to win the inaugural Olympic triathlon to give Canada its first gold, and Daniel Nestor and Sebastien Lareau teamed up to shock the tennis world by winning gold in men's doubles. Canada's proudest moment, however, was saved for last, as Nigerian immigrant Daniel Igali, on the Games' final day, completed his improbable journey from impoverished youth to Canadian Olympic hero, which he capped by kissing the Canadian flag after winning gold in freestyle wrestling.

TOP: Emilie Heymans and Anne Montminy captured one of four diving medals for Canada, a silver in women's synchronized 10m platform. BOTTOM: Daniel Igali (right) wrestled for gold for his adopted country on the Games' final day.

vicRAUTER

REMEMBERS

❝ Sandra Schmirler was one of this country's best curlers in the modern era. Multiple championships, Canadian, World Championships and of course, the gold medal in Nagano in '98. Again it's one of those sad stories, you wonder why it happens to people. She was going to be commentating for a network and we knew that she'd been sick. They discovered the tumor after the birth of her second child. It was a stubborn tumour and despite the treatments it moved quickly through her body. I remember that she wanted a comeback and I can remember the raspy voice at the news conference saying, "I'm going to be back, I'm going to work as a colour commentator." And she was there with her hat on because she had no hair left. And then in a matter of days she had passed. But she really was, again, one of those unique people who just captured the heart of this country. Didn't matter whether you were a curler or not, people knew of Sandra Schmirler. And now of course, the legacy of her is the foundation for babies who are in critical care and it supports neonatal centres across the country. She was really a very special lady. ❞

Diagnosed with a form of cancer known as metastatic adeno carcinoma shortly after the birth of her second child, curling great Sandra Schmirler's health deteriorated quickly. While working as a commentator for the Canadian National Junior Curling Championships in Moncton in 2000, she held a press conference to speak publicly about her struggle.

New York Yankees pitcher Roger Clemens throws a perfect strike — but with a broken bat — taking aim at New York Mets catcher Mike Piazza.

BAT OUT OF HELL
The Clemens–Piazza Feud Marks the New York Subway World Series

The natural rivalry between the New York Mets and the New York Yankees was made all the more intense after the personal feud that developed between Mets catcher Mike Piazza and Yankees star pitcher Roger Clemens earlier in the season.

The crosstown rivals had faced each other in interleague play in July, a series that featured Clemens hitting Piazza in the head with a high fastball that left the Mets catcher with a concussion. The ensuing trash talk only added to the drama of the first New York Subway World Series since 1956 between the two-time defending champion Yankees and the Mets, back in the Series for the first time since their win over Boston in 1986.

Game 1 was a Series classic that saw the Yankees tie the game in the ninth inning and win it in the 12th.

But the real fireworks went off in Game 2 when Piazza broke his bat fouling off a Clemens offering. The barrel of the bat rolled out to the mound, where Clemens retrieved it. What happened next perplexed everyone watching. Even the most ardent of Yankees supporters were mystified when Clemens picked up the broken bat and inexplicably threw it toward Piazza, who was running toward first base. The surreal scene nearly turned WWE as both players started toward each other, only to be separated by their respective teams spilling out of the dugouts. The Yankees, despite a five-run outburst by the Mets in the top of the ninth that included a Piazza homer, hung on for a 6–5 win. The teams split Games 3 and 4 before the Yankees capped off a World Series three-peat with a late-innings' win at Shea Stadium in Game 5.

2001

Ezra Shaw/Allsport

Up against the New York Yankees and the

WORLD SERIES TAKES BACK SEAT TO 9/11

Start of World Series Delayed by Terrorist Attack in New York

Delayed when regular-season games in September had to be postponed in the wake of 9/11, Game 1 of the World Series didn't take place until October 27.

The Arizona Diamondbacks, in only their fourth season, faced the three-time defending champion New York Yankees. But the Diamondbacks literally had a pair of aces up their sleeves in star pitchers Randy Johnson and Curt Schilling.

Giving up only three hits, Schilling and the D-Backs were easy 9-1 winners in Game 1. Not to be outdone, Johnson pitched a complete game shutout in Game 2, a 4-0 triumph.

Before Game 3, President George W. Bush threw out the ceremonial first pitch wearing a sweatshirt emblazoned with "FDNY," in honour of the New York Fire Department that performed so heroically on September 11. Bush threw a perfect strike and left the mound to chants of "U-S-A, U-S-A." Yankees starter Roger Clemens picked up where Bush left off, giving up only three hits and striking out nine in seven innings. The Yankees took the game 4–3 and also won Game 4 by a single run on Derek Jeter's 10th-inning, past midnight, solo home run, the first World Series homer hit in November. Game 5 featured similar dramatics. Yankee Scott Brosius tied the game

with a two-run homer with two out in the ninth, and Alfonso Soriano won it with a single in the bottom of the 12th.

The "Bronx Bombers" looked poised for a fourth straight championship when the Series returned to Arizona. But an offensive outburst, including an eight-run third, gave Johnson and the D-Backs an easy 15–2 win in Game 6.

Game 7 featured two 20-game winners, Schilling and Clemens, and was the pitching duel most expected through five scoreless innings. Arizona struck first in the bottom of the sixth, but the Yankees responded with one run in the seventh and another in the eighth courtesy of an Alfonso Soriano homer off Schilling. Arizona manager Bob Brenly surprised many by calling on Randy Johnson, who had thrown 104 pitches 24 hours earlier, to relieve Schilling. But the move paid off

...emotional weight of 9/11, the Arizona Diamondbacks captured the first November World Series in history.

as the "Big Unit" retired four Yankee batters in a row.

In the bottom of the ninth, the D-Backs had to face the game's best closer, Mariano Rivera, who had dropped his post-season ERA to 0.70 when he struck out the side in the eighth. But Rivera was normally a one-inning reliever. A series of mistakes and some bad luck soon put players on first and second. With one out, Tony Womack stroked a double that tied the game. Rivera's problems were about to get worse. After hitting Craig Counsell to load the bases, Rivera found himself facing Luis Gonzalez, the owner of 57 regular-season home runs. But the D-Backs needed one run, not four. And when Gonzalez hit a bloop that dropped into centre field, the Diamondbacks had captured the first and only November World Series in baseball history.

ROD**SMITH**

REMEMBERS

❝ Of all of my years working in a sports newsroom, that was the most unforgettable day because, for a period of time, sports was no longer relevant. It just didn't matter. The only worthy debate that morning was whether we should even do a show. Many of us didn't want to. There was a feeling that it might be disrespectful. We couldn't imagine anyone watching, anyway. After a lengthy debate, we concluded that the sports world isn't just about fun and games, big money contracts and managing salary caps. It's also about people — human beings with jobs to do, families to feed and dreams to chase. On the morning of September 11th, two of the people who boarded a plane in Boston were scouts with the Los Angeles Kings. Garnett "Ace" Bailey and Mark Bavis were on the way to L.A. for the start of training camp. They never made it. We led our show that evening with news of their deaths. Not just sports figures. People. Victims of a terrible tragedy. Even as a sports channel, we served a purpose on a day when sports didn't matter. In my opinion, it was the most difficult show we've ever done. But it was the right decision to do it. ❞

TSN THAT'S HOCKEY

RAY'S REWARD

Colorado Avalanche Defenceman Ray Bourque's Cup Runneth Over . . . Finally

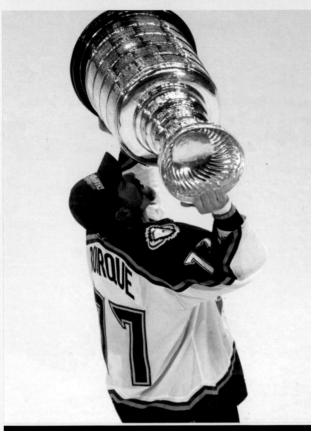

Ray Bourque hoists the Stanley Cup for
the first time.

Brian Bahr/Allsport

PIERRE McGUIRE

REMEMBERS

" It was a phenomenal accomplishment. Knowing how close he was in Boston on a couple of occasions only to run into two very good teams in Edmonton and Pittsburgh. You just felt so good for a person that played so well for so long to finally get it done. I remember the relief on his face when he was holding the Cup. It said "I got to the top of the mountain." It really said it all. "

From the time the Boston Bruins selected him in the first round of the NHL Entry Draft in 1979, Ray Bourque steadily set about compiling one of the most impressive resumés in hockey history: five Norris Trophies as the league's top defenceman, 19 All-Star Game appearances, 21 playoff seasons and career scoring marks for defencemen: 410 goals, 1579 points. The only thing missing was a Stanley Cup.

Bourque had come close, losing two Stanley Cup finals (1988 and 1990) to the Edmonton Oilers. But by 1999, the Bruins had fallen on hard times. And Bourque, at age 39 and with nearly 1700 games under his belt, was running out of time.

No. 77 was a legend in Boston, where he had played for 21 seasons. Unfortunately, in that time, he had also earned the title of the "The Greatest Player Never to Have Won the Cup." As the 2000 trade deadline approached, the loyal (to a fault, some would say) Bourque asked the Bruins to move him to a team that had a chance to win it all. On March 6, he was traded to the Colorado Avalanche, a perennial Cup contender since they won hockey's greatest prize in 1996. The "Win One for Ray" campaign fell short that year, as Colorado bowed out to Detroit in a seven-game Western Conference final. But Bourque was back in the lineup in 2000–01 for what many believed would be a final try at a championship. Before the playoffs began, Bourque outfitted his teammates with "Mission 16W" caps, signifying the number of wins a team needed to win it all.

Fourteen wins later, the mission was in peril. The Avalanche trailed the defending Cup champion New Jersey Devils 3–2 in the final. But a 4–0 road win sent the series back to Colorado for the penultimate game. Bourque had tears in his eyes as the national anthem played before the game, and again as the clock ticked down on a 3–1 Avalanche win. Instead of following tradition and hoisting the Cup first, captain Joe Sakic passed the Stanley Cup to Ray Bourque before hoisting it himself. Nobody seemed to mind; they were too busy chanting, "Ray, Ray, Ray." "Mission 16W" was over, and new caps reading "77 Mission Accomplished" were passed around the victorious team's champagne-soaked dressing room.

REMEMBERS

PITCHER DANNY ALMONTE GOES 4-0 FOR THE RONANDO PAULINO TEAM AT THE LITTLE LEAGUE WORLD SERIES. DOCUMENTS WOULD LATER SHOW HE WAS TWO YEARS TOO OLD TO COMPETE.

❝ When the Danny Almonte situation occurred I remember feeling that it was more of a disappointment than a surprise. We had suspected that this might be taking place for a while, that some teams might be bringing in players, especially pitchers, who were perhaps a little older than they should be. But he was an exceptional case because he was just tearing through the Little League World Series and also seemed a little bigger than the other kids.

It was like when Mark McGwire and Sammy Sosa were pounding out all of those home runs and you thought, "Man, McGwire's forearms are huge. And Sosa used to be so skinny. But I'm sure it's nothing. Baseball's so great again, I'm so happy everyone's watching the sport after the strike." And then, of course, it all came crashing down.

It was exactly the same with Danny Almonte. The feeling was, "Wow, this kid could be a Cy Young winner some day. But, oh, wait. He's two years older than every other kid on the field." So that's pretty much what we thought in the newsroom at the time. It started out as a feel good story but, unfortunately, ended up making everyone feel bad in the end. **❞**

Barry Bonds passed Mark McGwire to capture the single-season home-run title, ending the year with 73 dingers.

Harry How/Allsport

BONDS ECLIPSES McGWIRE

San Francisco Giants Slugger Breaks Single-Season Home-Run Record

It took 37 years for someone to break New York Yankee Roger Maris's single-season record of 61 home runs. Few baseball fans expected that a new mark would be established so soon afterwards. Barry Bonds had long established himself as one of the game's best hitters. But the San Francisco Giants star had always been about more than home runs, almost always hitting for average and, early in his career, stealing bases too. Before 2000, when he hit 49, his best home-run total was 46, in 1993.

That all changed in 2001 when Bonds burst out of the starting gates swinging. He smashed 11 homers in April, an amazing 17 in May and 11 more in June. He slowed down in July, when he hit only six round-trippers, but when he hit 12 more in August, the Bonds home-run watch was back on full-time. By the end of September, a month in which he clouted 12 more homers, Bonds's season total sat at 69, one short of Mark McGwire's mark of 70 set in 1998. And he still had eight games to play.

Bonds went homer-less over the next four games, and suddenly there were doubts about what had seemed like a sure thing only days before. The record-tying homer, in Game 159, was a gargantuan 480-foot, ninth-inning shot off of Astros pitcher Wilfredo Rodriguez at Houston's Enron Field.

The next day, back at San Francisco's Pac Bell Park, in a game against the rival Dodgers that the Giants needed to win, Bonds broke the record in the bottom of the first and added some insurance, hitting number 72 in the third inning of a losing cause. He added number 73 two days later. The ownership of the ball later became the subject of a legal dispute, and the ball was ordered by a judge to be sold at auction, where it was purchased for $450,000.

Bonds continued to be one of the game's greatest home-run hitters in the seasons that followed — albeit, amidst much controversy as details emerged of him being among the many baseball players implicated in the steroid scandal.

A LEGEND DIES AT DAYTONA

Dale Earnhardt Has Fatal Crash in Race's Final Turn

Robert Laberge/Allsport

"Undoubtedly this is one of the toughest announcements I've personally had to make. After the accident in Turn 4 at the end of the Daytona 500, we've lost Dale Earnhardt."

— NASCAR president Mike Helton

Dale Earnhardt was posthumously inducted into both the Motorsports Hall of Fame of America and the International Motorsports Hall of Fame.

Jamie Squire/Allsport

As soon as their cars slid to a stop, Kenny Schrader
The angle of impact and the speed that

They didn't call Dale Earnhardt "The Intimidator" for nothing. NASCAR racing's biggest star always said that when it came time to race, his son Dale Jr. was just another competitor to him — one to be passed, and maybe even bumped, if he ever got in the way. Driving in his 23rd Daytona 500, which he had won in 1998 after 20 years of disappointment, Earnhardt was also the owner of a NASCAR team, Dale Earnhardt Inc., though he continued to race for Richard Childress Racing.

climbed out of his yellow Pontiac and walked to Dale Earnhardt's car before calling for paramedics. Earnhardt was travelling at made for a lethal combination.

In the race's final lap, Earnhardt found himself fighting for third place behind DEI racers Michael Waltrip and Dale Jr., running first and second respectively. Earnhardt appeared to back off the leaders, content to protect them from racers Sterling Marlin, Rusty Wallace and Ken Schrader coming in fast behind them. Going into Turn 4, Earnhardt continued to block, while Marlin appeared to make his move. The two cars, travelling approximately 180 miles an hour, bumped, sending Earnhardt's famous No. 3 black Chevy crashing into a concrete retaining wall, then into the path of Schrader's car.

After crossing the finish line, second-place finisher Dale Jr. leapt from his car, anxious for news about his father. But the news was not good. Indeed, it was the worst news possible. Dale Earnhardt, the seven-time NASCAR Winston Cup champion, was pronounced dead on arrival at the hospital, having succumbed almost immediately to injuries caused by the initial crash.

2002

Team Canada's women cried tears of joy after their emotional win over the United States

THE KINGS AND QUEENS OF THE ICE

Canada's Women Regain Hockey Gold at the Salt Lake City 2002 Winter Games

After losing to their arch-rivals, the United States, the Canadian women's hockey team had to settle for silver at the Nagano 1998 Olympic Winter Games. Hopes for gold at the Salt Lake City 2002 Winter Games were high, but following eight straight losses to the U.S. team in pre-Olympic tournament play, there were doubts too. The Canadian men, on the other hand, looking to end a 50-year gold drought, had a pair of weapons to help them in their quest — one loonie secret and a magnificent leader whom everyone knew all about.

The Canadian women steamrolled through the opening round, outscoring the opposition 25–0 in three games. And thanks to five unanswered goals in the third period of their semifinal against Finland, Canada was off to

in hockey at the 2002 Winter Games.

Olympic champions from the Czech Republic on deck, hand-wringing took over from hockey as Canada's national sport ... for a little while anyway. But Canada responded with their best effort against the Czechs. After sitting out the previous game, crafty Canadian captain Mario Lemieux scored twice to lead the way in a 3–3 tie. Following what he perceived as the mistreatment of his players, an uncharacteristically irate Canadian general manager Wayne Gretzky issued Canada's rallying cry. "I know the whole world wants us to lose, except for Canada and Canada fans," he said. "But we'll be there, we'll be standing."

Team Canada got a huge break before they faced Finland in the quarter-finals. In one of the greatest upsets in Olympic hockey history, underdog Belarus eliminated Sweden on a long shot that Swedish goalie Tommy Salo misplayed. With one of their chief rivals now out of the tournament, an inspired Team Canada outshot Finland 34–19 on their way to a 2–1 win. An easy 7–1 win over Belarus then set up a gold-medal showdown against the United States, who had defeated Russia in the other semifinal.

With the score 1–0 in favour of the United States early in the championship game, Lemieux turned things around for Canada . . . without ever touching the puck. He deftly opened his legs to let a long pass sail though them and onto the stick of teammate Paul Kariya, who fired the tying goal past U.S. goalie Mike Richter. A Jarome Iginla goal late in the first gave Canada a 2–1 lead after 20 minutes. The teams traded goals in the second, but Canadian goalie Martin Brodeur held off the hard-pressing Americans in the third. Iginla's second of the game and a brilliant individual effort by Joe Sakic gave Canada a 5–2 lead and, ultimately, gold.

While Lemieux circled the ice with a Canadian flag, Gretzky headed for the centre-ice faceoff circle, where he dug out a $1 Canadian coin, placed there by the tournament's Canadian ice maker before the start of the Games for good luck. Only the truly superstitious can believe that the "Lucky Loonie," as it came to be known, affected the golden outcome, but it certainly didn't hurt, as Canada won men's hockey gold for the first time since 1952.

CANADA'S MARIO LEMIEUX CHANGES THE PACE OF THE GOLD MEDAL GAME AGAINST THE UNITED STATES WITHOUT EVEN TOUCHING THE PUCK.

❝ I was in the studio with Bob McKenzie and Gord Miller when that play happened and we all said at the same time, "Lemieux did that on purpose." There was a ton of emotion involved for many reasons and obviously with everything being so wrong in Nagano. And then Mario, a guy who comes out of retirement having beaten cancer, comes to the Olympics and is the captain. You had the line of Simon Gagné, Joe Sakic and Jarome Iginla, who were so great together. And Brodeur replacing Curtis Joseph. There are so many stories from that Olympics and from that game but that play is one of those stand-alone moments that you will always remember. You'll always remember where you were when that happened.

And it was incredible to watch. The play is going a million miles an hour and you have to process that information instantly. It just shows you the creative genius of Mario, and the ability of Paul Kariya to basically read Mario's mind. Watching it happen, I'm not even sure a computer could do it so quickly. ❞

the gold medal game against the Americans . . . again.

Despite being called for nine minor penalties by an American referee, the Canadians led 3–1 after two periods, the key goal a breakaway marker by Canadian forward Jayna Hefford that trickled across the goal line with only one second left in the middle frame. The U.S. team argued that the play was offside at their blueline, but the backbreaker stood. Canada took four more penalties in the third, and American Karyn Bye narrowed the gap to 3–2, but the Canadians hung on for golden glory.

Unlike the women, the Canadian men stumbled out of the gate, absorbing a 5–2 pasting at the hands of Sweden in the opener and then holding on to edge lowly Germany 3–2. With the defending

Adrian Dennis/AFP/Getty Images

SILVER TURNS TO GOLD

Pairs Figure Skaters Jamie Salé and David Pelletier Are Redeemed

Jamie Salé and David Pelletier were golden for Canada in pairs figure skating but only after a "silver-lining" decision resulting from protest and a media storm.

Clive Brunskill/Getty Images

Rarely has figure skating been more prominent than it was at the Olympic Winter Games in Salt Lake City. But once again, it was for all the wrong reasons. A scandal erupted that rocked not only the Canadian Olympic Association, but all of sports. The Canadian pairs tandem of Jamie Salé and David Pelletier was right in the middle of it, and when it was all said and done, they would become international heroes.

Although Salé and Pelletier would turn in the greatest skates of their lives, and perhaps the greatest in Olympic history, they knew something was awry when they looked up at their scores. They had received ridiculously low marks for artistic impression and would have to settle for silver, with gold going to Russian pair Elena Berezhnaya and Anton Sikharulidze. The crowd, suspecting foul play, booed heartily. Later, Salé broke down in tears as the silver medal was placed around her neck. The chain of events that followed next would span the globe.

The controversial result, witnessed by millions on television around the world, turned Salé and Pelletier into stars overnight. From Jay Leno to Larry King to Canadian Prime Minister Jean Chrétien, everyone was talking about the Canadian duo being denied their golden dream. And while the cry was strong, the pair and their Canadian fans were resigned to their fate. Nobody was holding their breath waiting for the scores to be overturned.

However, all the attention the pair received would work in their favour. An investigation by the International Skating Union (ISU) led to the revelation by the French skating federation that judge Marie-Reine Le Gougne had been pressured to vote for the Russians over the Canadians. The ISU took the unprecedented step of awarding a second set of gold medals to the Canadian pair. On February 17, six days after they were robbed of gold, Salé and Pelletier stood at the top of the podium to finally bask in their golden moment.

BRIAN WILLIAMS

REMEMBERS

❝ The best thing that happened to Jamie and David was that the Games were in the United States. There was no question that the International Olympic Committee was embarrassed by this. Every time they went somewhere it was on the front page of the papers, every time they turned on a television set—from David Letterman to Jay Leno—they were bombarded by it. You really didn't have to be a Canadian or know anything about figure skating to know that this was wrong. The IOC felt something had to be done, and they moved like they've never moved before. That was accomplished due to the strong leadership provided by Dr. Jacques Rogge in his first Olympics as president of the IOC. **❞**

Henri Szwarc/Bongarts/Getty Images

SCOTTY GOES FOR A FINAL SKATE

Coaching Legend Laces 'Em Up for Final Spin with Stanley

Scotty Bowman adapted with each and every generation of hockey players he coached from when he first stepped behind an NHL bench in 1966 until he retired in 2002 after a ninth Stanley Cup and 1,244 coaching wins.

Many had suspected Bowman would retire following the 2002 play-offs, especially if Detroit won the Cup. When the Red Wings swept the Carolina Hurricanes, he removed any doubt. He disappeared from the Wings' bench in the final moments of the game, only to reappear during on-ice celebrations wearing his skates.

The dean of NHL head coaches, who was deprived of the chance to play in the NHL because of a head injury he received in junior hockey, seized his final opportunity, at age 68, to do what he had done in 1997, and what millions of hockey players have dreamed of doing — skating around an NHL rink with the Stanley Cup lifted over his head. Bowman's ninth Stanley Cup win had allowed him to surpass one of his mentors, Montreal legend Toe Blake, for the most Cups in an NHL coaching career. Still on his skates, with nothing left to prove, Bowman formally announced his retirement, leaving the job, and the game, he loved so much.

After guiding so many players to hockey's ultimate prize, legendary coach Scotty Bowman takes a turn with the Stanley Cup himself.

Dave Sandford/Getty Images/NHLI

SAKU'S TRIUMPHANT RETURN

Captain Koivu's Comeback from Cancer Lifts Habs

W hen Montreal Canadiens captain Saku Koivu was diagnosed with non–Hodgkin's lymphoma before the 2001–02 season, doctors gave him a 50–50 chance of surviving the next five years. Koivu's chances of playing hockey that year were thought to be worse.

There were cheers and tears when Koivu appeared at the Canadiens home opener in October, walking behind the team bench in his Habs jersey. But there were concerns too. He appeared thin, and he was completely hairless thanks to his chemotherapy treatments.

Six months later, after eight cycles of chemotherapy and 79 NHL games missed, Koivu was pronounced fit to return to the Habs, who were fighting for one of the final Eastern Conference playoff spots. And on April 9, he was on Molson Centre ice as the team prepared to face the Ottawa Senators. Koivu was slated to play on the fourth line that night, but Habs coach Michel Therrien had slotted him in to take the opening faceoff, which meant he was standing on the Canadiens blueline waiting to be introduced as part of the starting lineup. When house announcer Michel Lacroix called his name, the Montreal fans gave Koivu a standing ovation that lasted a full eight minutes. Lacroix tried to interrupt three times, and three times he was drowned out. There wasn't a dry eye in the house. "I've never seen anything like it," said Koivu's teammate Doug Gilmour, a 19-year NHL veteran. "And it's something I hope I never see again."

The Canadiens used the 4–3 win over Ottawa and the emotion of Koivu's return not only to secure a spot in the playoffs, but to upset the top-ranked Boston Bruins in the Eastern Conference quarterfinals. Koivu survived an extremely physical first period in the first game in Boston and helped lead the eighth-place Habs to a surprising 5–2 defeat of the Bruins, whose 101 regular-season points were

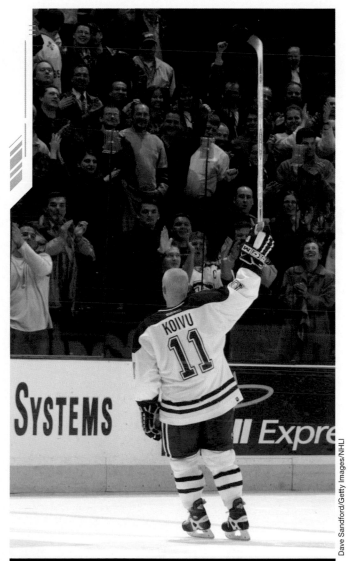

Saku Koivu's return after fighting cancer will go down as one of hockey's most emotional moments.

second in the NHL only to Detroit. In Game 3 back in Montreal, with the Canadiens down 3–1 after two periods, Koivu notched the game winner to give the Habs a 2–1 series lead. By the time Montreal had eliminated Boston 4–2, Koivu had collected seven points. At season's end, he was named the winner of the Bill Masterton Memorial Trophy, the award handed out to an NHL player who best exemplifies perseverance, sportsmanship and a dedication to hockey.

2003

TV TOP10 MOMENTS

1 Mike Weir becomes the first Canadian to win a major, capturing the Masters on the first hole of a sudden-death playoff vs. Len Mattiace.

2 The Chicago Cubs are five outs from making the World Series when fan Steve Bartman interferes with Moises Alou's attempt to catch a Florida foul ball. The extra chance opens the door for a Marlin comeback and Florida wins Games 6 and 7.

3 Vancouver is awarded the 2010 Winter Games with a three-vote win over Pyeongchang, South Korea.

4 Boston's Pedro Martinez pushes New York Yankee 72-year-old bench coach Don Zimmer to the ground when benches clear during Game 3 of the ALCS.

5 Canadiens' goalie José Théodore is the face (and toque) of the first outdoor classic, as Montreal and Edmonton face off in freezing temperatures at Commonwealth Stadium.

6 Aaron Boone hits a walk-off home run against Boston in the 11th inning, sending the New York Yankees to the World Series.

7 Annika Sorenstam plays the Colonial, becoming the first woman to play on the PGA Tour since 1945. She misses the cut.

8 In response to charges he sexually assaulted a 19-year-old woman in Colorado, Kobe Bryant says at a press conference, "I didn't force her to do anything against her will. I'm innocent."

9 Vince Carter gives up his starting spot to Michael Jordan during introductions of the NBA All-Star Game.

10 A day after his father dies, Green Bay's Brett Favre passes for 399 yards and four TDs vs. Oakland.

Mike Weir found himself in prestigious company as Masters champ, joining the likes of Tiger

A GREEN JACKET FOR MIKE

Canadian Mike Weir Wins Masters

Mike Weir led the 2003 Masters after 36 holes, but a 75 on Saturday dropped him two strokes behind the leader, Jeff Maggert, heading into Sunday. But the lefty from Bright's Grove, Ontario, was no stranger to come-from-behind victories, having previously won five tournaments when going into the final round.

Weir didn't let himself get distracted by his poor Saturday showing. Instead, he approached the final round with the same mindset as he had the first three. He had a plan of attack for each of Augusta National's 18 holes, and he was sticking with it.

The plan paid off almost immediately. His birdie on the second hole and a triple bogey by Maggert on the third hole put Weir back in the lead. But while Maggert started to fade, long-shot Len Mattiace, playing four pairings ahead of Weir and Maggert, put on a charge that at one point gave him a three-shot advantage.

But Weir was unfazed. When he birdied the 15th hole at the same time Mattiace was tapping in for bogey at 18, the two men were tied atop the leader board.

On the 18th, Weir had a long birdie putt for the win, a putt he left six feet short of the cup. He later called the en-

Woods in the green jacket club.

Weir was the first lefty in four decades to win a major title.

suing par putt the biggest of his life. But with a quiet confidence Weir quickly and calmly knocked in the putt to send the Masters to a playoff.

The playoff had none of the drama of the holes that came before. A double bogey by Mattiace left the door wide open for Weir, who would need only to two-putt from about four feet to make him the first-ever Canadian to put on the coveted green jacket and the first left-hander in 40 years to win a major. Canadians, including golf-crazy Prime Minister Jean Chrétien, rejoiced.

Twenty-four hours later, Canada's newest folk hero received a standing ovation as he dropped the puck at a Maple Leafs game in Toronto. For days, his face was everywhere, his name on everyone's lips.

"This win is a win for me and my family," Weir recognized when it was all over. "But it is a big win for Canada."

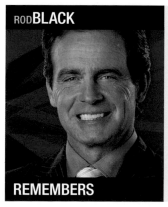

ROD**BLACK**

REMEMBERS

66 I remember I was with Vijay Singh and Freddie Couples, and a couple of other guys, watching the final hole on TV. I'll always recall when Mike sunk the final putt on 18 — which was a 5- or 6-footer — to send it to a playoff, the players started standing up. We were all witnessing the final piece in the evolution of Mike Weir's rise from potential contender to major champion and the face of golf in Canada. And when Mike got the jacket from Tiger Woods, I thought it was a special moment. There were so many Canadians at Augusta that day, and they were just wired for him. It was something to behold. 99

Canada gets its second Winter Games — and third overall — with the awarding of the 2010 Winter Olympics to Vancouver/Whistler. Some high-profile Canadians supported the bid, including Wayne Gretzky, Prime Minister Jean Chrétien, Olympian Catriona Le May Doan and Whistler Mayor Hugh O'Reilly.

Michal Ruzicka/AFP/Getty Images

LET THE GAMES BEGIN!

Vancouver Wins Gold in Bid to Host 2010 Winter Games

Canada Day might be the 1st of July, but it was on July 2 when the nation rejoiced with the news that the Olympic Winter Games would be returning to Canada.

Vancouver 2010 had been more than five years in the making, as a dedicated team spent the previous half-decade turning a city's Olympic dream into reality. When it came time for the final presentation during an International Olympic Committee (IOC) session in Prague, Czech Republic, Canada had an ace up its sleeve, or rather a lucky loonie in its pocket. The Vancouver delegation remembers carrying the Canadian dollar for luck. Lady Luck was smiling on Vancouver, as the city of Salzburg, Austria, thought

to be Vancouver's main rival, was eliminated on the first ballot by voting IOC members. The final decision came down to Vancouver and Pyeongchang, South Korea, which had surprisingly fallen only three votes short of hosting the Games on the first ballot. However, once all the votes were tabulated, Vancouver would win, and the countdown was on for Canada to host its third Olympic Games.

TSN, a part of Canada's Olympic Broadcast Media Consortium, heads to Vancouver for unparalleled coverage of the 2010 Olympic Winter Games. As an Official Broadcaster, TSN will deliver 304 hours of live coverage, all in HD, over the 17 days of competition.

BRIAN WILLIAMS

REMEMBERS

❝ I was in Prague and there was an eruption in the room when the winning bid was announced. We also had the live feed from Vancouver and Whistler and saw the celebrations. We hadn't realized how close the voting was. It was an exceptional bid presented by VANOC, and it was supported by the presence of Wayne Gretzky and Prime Minister Jean Chrétien, who was brilliant. Vancouver will be the biggest city to host the Winter Games, bigger than Calgary and bigger than Salt Lake, and visitors will absolutely love it and love Whistler. ❞

TURNING POINT

THE BILLY GOAT CURSE AND STEVE BARTMAN

The Chicago Cubs Curse Continues as an Infamous Fan Spoils the World Series Party

Five outs away from their first World Series appearance since 1945, the Chicago Cubs experienced the unthinkable. The loveable losers who had put their fans through years of misery had the National League pennant ripped out of their grasp by someone who had shared their pain. In the blink of an eye, Steve Bartman, a lifelong Cubs fan, a man who devoted his time to coaching Little League baseball in Chicago, became public enemy number one.

The Cubs went into the eighth inning of Game 6 of the NL Championship Series leading the Florida Marlins 3–0. It appeared that the Billy Goat Curse, placed on the team by a man who was forced to take his goat and leave Wrigley Stadium in the 1945 Series, was about to be exorcised. With one out and a runner on second, Cubs pitcher Mark Prior induced Florida's Luis Castillo to hit a high foul pop-up toward the left-field stands. Cubs left fielder Moisés Alou raced over, appearing to have a play on the ball for the second out. But Bartman, and several other fans, tried to catch themselves a playoff souvenir. The ball bounced off Bartman's hand, sending Alou into a fury. And he wasn't the only one. Bartman was escorted from the ballpark for his own safety.

After that, the Cubs simply fell apart. Walks, errors, a wild pitch and some timely hitting by the Marlins led to an eight-run Florida eighth and a win that sent the Series to Game 7. Grown men cried. And they cried again the next day when Florida took the deciding game before their very eyes at Wrigley Field. The Billy Goat Curse lived on, accidentally aided by a loyal Cubbies fan.

The famous ball was put on display before being blown up.

Jonathan Daniel/Getty Images

JAY ONRAIT REMEMBERS

" Fair or not, the incident with Steve Bartman is imprinted on all of our minds. That year, it looked like it could be the Cubs and Red Sox in the World Series, baseball's most cursed teams. And then both of them blew it in such painful ways.

I always find it funny when people criticize any fan for reaching up and trying to grab a baseball when it comes three or four feet into the stands, because that's just the instinct that we would all have, more to protect ourselves than anything else. To me, this has always been an overblown incident. Could Moisés Alou have caught the ball? Yes. Did the Cubs have plenty of opportunities to get out of that inning regardless of what happened on that play? Yes. I've always felt that it was more of a case of the Cubs losing their focus. To this day, it blows my mind that Steve Bartman was blamed so vehemently for that incident. He was clearly a hardcore baseball fan who just wanted to watch the game, and then reacted as most of us would have when a foul ball came his way. But now he can really never go to a Cubs game again in person. For the rest of his life, he'll be known as the guy who kept the curse going. "

" I think that despite the fact that the Alouettes lost to the Edmonton Eskimos in Regina, you could say that the image of Ben Cahoon stretched out, with one arm out reaching for that ball in traffic, for what was a crucial catch with his team down by two touchdowns early in the game — that was the lasting image of the 2003 Grey Cup. He was named Outstanding Canadian with close to 150 receiving yards in that game, and it also kind of personifies the great all-around receiver that Ben Cahoon is, the guy that pound for pound is as tough as they come, who can go over the middle make the catch in traffic, take a punishing, punishing blow, and bounce right back up. But this catch in the 2003 Grey Cup shows the finesse side of his game, and that he has great, great hands. "

Ben Cahoon is known for playing big and big plays. The Montreal Alouettes receiver will be forever known for his "handy" work in the 2003 Grey Cup.

HERITAGE CLASSIC TAKES HOCKEY BACK TO THE POND

Montreal Canadiens and Edmonton Oilers Play First Outdoor Game in NHL History

The NHL's first outdoor game was preceded by a mega-star showdown between Montreal and Edmonton dynasties, represented by the likes of "The Flower" and "The Great One."

Jeff Vinnick/Getty Images

Sixteen hours a day for two weeks, crews worked to turn Commonwealth Stadium in Edmonton into a hockey rink for a regular-season NHL game between the Montreal Canadiens and the Edmonton Oilers called the Heritage Classic.

First up, though, was the Megastars Game, which featured Hall of Fame rosters from two of the NHL's greatest dynasties, the Habs and the Oilers. The spotlight was saved, of course, for Wayne Gretzky, who was playing in his first post-retirement game, and Mark Messier, the lone active NHL player in the lineup, who joined his former Oilers comrades for the event. But with heavy snowfall and extreme cold in the forecast, playing both games was in doubt.

However, in the spirit of the Great White North, they did play, and in the strangest of scenarios. In the

Megastars matchup, Ken Linseman and Marty McSorley provided the offence for the Oilers while Hall of Famers like Gretzky and Lafleur handled the snow removal, literally. With exceptional play from Grant Fuhr and Bill Ranford, the Oilers pulled off a 2–0 victory.

"We really felt like we were 10 years old again," Lafleur said. "With the legs of a 50-year-old!"

It was then time for the main event. With game-time temperatures dipping to -20° Celsius, the players did their best to stay warm, including skating short shifts to get back to their heated benches and José Théodore famously sporting a toque atop his Habs goalie mask. The Habs jumped out to a 3–1 lead and held off the Oilers for a 4–3 win before 56,000-plus brave, shivering fans and millions more toasty-warm television viewers.

CHAPTER FIVE

2004–2008

A SILVER ANNIVERSARY

Between 2004 and 2008, TSN had matured and was setting a new standard for sports broadcasting in Canada — including being the first Canadian network to deliver a daily newscast in high definition.

Overall, TSN's audiences had skyrocketed, led by its impressive schedule of NHL, NFL and NBA games — along with acquiring exclusive broadcast rights to all CFL games, including the Grey Cup. In 2008, the network launched TSN2 to give sports fans even more coverage of live sporting events.

The sports world, however, didn't experience the same smooth ascendance between 2004 and 2008. It was a period of truly extreme highs and lows. Just as long championship droughts were broken and legendary records were felled, baseball and many other sports were plagued with talk of steroids and cheating. For every Tiger Woods, there was a Barry Bonds. For every inspiring performance by the likes of Rafael Nadal, Steve Nash and Sidney Crosby, there was dogfighting, violence and gambling. Canadians would celebrate their most decorated Olympic champion ever in the same year that their national hockey team shocked the nation by failing to win a medal.

Through it all, the growing roster at TSN stuck to the game plan of bringing the stories home, to Canadians.

Vladimir Rys/Bongarts/Getty Images

Canadian speed skater Cindy Klassen's smile lit up the nation after she captured gold in the 1500 metres, the fourth of her record five Olympic medals in Torino.

2004

TV TOP 10 MOMENTS

1 Vancouver's Todd Bertuzzi skates up behind Colorado's Steve Moore, punches him in the side of the head and shoves him to the ice, causing career-ending injuries for Moore. Bertuzzi pleads guilty in a plea bargain agreement to assault.

2 In the final minute of an NBA game in Detroit, Indiana's Ron Artest and Stephen Jackson charge into the stands to fight with fans.

3 Blood soaks through the sock of Boston's Curt Schilling, the result of a right ankle injury, as the pitcher beats St. Louis in Game 2 of the World Series.

4 The puck goes off Martin Gélinas's skate and appears to cross the goal line, but it's ruled a no-goal for Calgary and Tampa Bay goes on to win Game 6 of the Stanley Cup final.

5 Mike Weir loses on the third sudden-death playoff hole to Vijay Singh at the Canadian Open.

6 Canadian goalie Marc-André Fleury's clearing attempt goes into his own net, giving the U.S. a lead and gold at the World Junior Championship.

7 Pre-race Canadian favourite Perdita Felicien hits the first hurdle and falls in the Olympic 100-metre final.

8 Todd Bertuzzi expresses remorse and cries at a press conference called for him to address the Steve Moore incident.

9 Phil Mickelson makes an 18-foot birdie putt on the 18th to win the Masters by one shot and earn his first green jacket.

10 Paul McCallum misses an 18-yard field goal in overtime in the Western Conference final and Saskatchewan loses to B.C.

After watching their team lose the Stanley Cup final to the Tampa Bay Lightning, Calgary

FLAMES UNLIKELY CUP RUN

Calgary Fans Fuel Flames Unlikely Cup Run

Few picked the sixth-seeded Calgary Flames to make much noise in the 2004 Stanley Cup playoffs. But Martin Gélinas's overtime winner in Game 7 against Vancouver in the first round sparked the Flames to one of the most unlikely Stanley Cup runs in recent memory.

After the win in Vancouver, Calgary came up against the powerhouse Detroit Red Wings, the top seed in the Western Conference and a team built to win it all. Inspired by Cup-starved Calgary fans gaining a league-wide reputation for their fervour, the Flames provided more overtime heroics, with Gélinas again delivering the series-winning goal in overtime.

In the Western Conference final, Calgary traded pairs of road wins with the second-seeded San Jose Sharks

Flames fans came out by the thousands to celebrate the team's exciting and unlikely run.

PIERRE McGUIRE

REMEMBERS

“ It was amazing. I remember just how physically devastating they were as a team. They were the best team in the league at that time at the old rules. And of course, Miikka Kiprusoff was a big part of why they were there. One of the things that helped them was they played Vancouver in the first round and Todd Bertuzzi had been suspended for the hit on Steve Moore. Once they got through that first series, you could see that they were a very different animal. Their depth guys like Craig Conroy and Marcus Nillson were just very tough to play against, and obviously Jarome Iginla was just so good at that time. But again, Kiprusoff was a huge difference.

The city of Calgary was wild. The Red Mile was awesome and the fan base in Calgary was electrifying. Just walking around the city, everybody was wearing a Flames sweater or a big red cowboy hat with a big 'C' on it. I remember Conservative leader Stephen Harper came by our podium to say hello. Everybody wanted to get on the Flames bandwagon. ”

before goaltender Miikka Kiprusoff shut the door, leading the Flames to a shutout win in Game 5 and a 3–1 victory to win the series in six and bring the Stanley Cup final back to Canada. The entire city was in a frenzy as 17th Avenue was transformed into "The Red Mile," with thousands of fans celebrating every game. Standing in Calgary's way was an equally unlikely opponent: the Tampa Bay Lightning.

The teams traded 4–1 wins in Games 1 and 2, then swapped shutouts in Games 3 and 4. In Game 5, overtime magic took over once again as Oleg Saprykin delivered the winner for the Flames, who took a 3–2 series lead. Game 6 in Calgary had all the drama anyone could hope for. After Gélinas missed scoring the winner in regula-

tion by mere inches on a puck that deflected off his skate, the game went to overtime.

The Flames, their fans, the entire city of Calgary was just one goal away from the Stanley Cup, but it wasn't meant to be. When Martin St. Louis scored the winner for the Lightning, both teams headed back to Florida for a winner-take-all Game 7 showdown.

Ruslan Fedotenko's pair of goals gave Tampa a 2–0 lead. The Flames responded in the third when Craig Conroy made it 2–1. But then a penalty to Andrew Ference with a minute left infuriated the Flames and put an end to Calgary's Stanley Cup quest.

Despite the loss, the Flames' amazing run was celebrated by 30,000 fans at a rally at Calgary's Olympic Plaza.

TURNING POINT

RED SOX BREAK BAMBINO CURSE

BoSox Win First World Series Since 1918

Joy was the emotion on display as Boston players celebrated first World Series title in 86 years.

It had been 86 years.

Al Bello/Getty Images

When the Boston Red Sox sold Babe Ruth to the New York Yankees in 1920, it marked the beginning of a great change in the baseball landscape. The Yankees, who had never won anything, would dominate the sport for the rest of the 20th century, winning 26 World Series. The Red Sox, who had won five of the first 16 World Series, would win no more. The Curse of the Bambino would haunt Boston fans for generations. But that all changed in 2004. And fittingly, it happened against the hated Yankees.

The Yanks had just beaten Boston 19–8 to take a commanding 3–0 game lead in the American League Championship Series. It appeared to be business as usual for both teams as New York took a one-run lead into the bottom of the ninth in Game 4, three outs from a sweep. And they had perhaps the game's finest closer, Mariano Rivera, on the mound.

But Rivera walked Kevin Millar, who was then replaced by pinch runner Dave Roberts. Roberts promptly stole

Elsa/Getty Images

their four-game sweep of the St. Louis Cardinals for the team's

second on Rivera and came home when Bill Mueller singled. The game was tied. That hit, off the usually untouchable Rivera, seemed to ignite something in the Red Sox. David Ortiz won the game for Boston with a home run in the 12th, and played hero again in Game 5 with a 14th-inning game-winning single. Red Sox starter Curt Schilling dominated Game 6, despite pitching through severe ankle pain. And in Game 7, it was Johnny Damon who hit a grand slam to help ensure Boston didn't lose their chance to break the curse and make history. Boston's 10–3 win in Game 7 made them the first team in baseball history to come back from a 3–0 series deficit. And it propelled them into the World Series.

The Series was something of an anticlimax as Boston swept St. Louis behind masterful pitching and timely hitting. For the first time since 1918, the Red Sox were the champions of baseball — the curse of the Bambino was broken.

ROD BLACK

REMEMBERS

❝ To get to the World Series is one thing, but to beat the Yankees, and to be down three games to nothing, that was the most amazing thing. I'm not one that has ever believed in curses. I'm not superstitious, but I do believe that sometimes teams, because they think there's something to that stuff, react differently. And this team didn't. This team, even down three-nothing, came rallying back. And that was just the American League Championship. Now, you still have to go win the World Series. But in fact it was just that they were a really, really good team. And you know people tried to play that curse of the Babe and all this. And this was one of those seminal moments in baseball history when a team is finally able to break a long drought. **❞**

TURNING POINT

THE BERTUZZI-MOORE INCIDENT
On-Ice Attack Shocks Sports World

The incident had been building for a couple of games. On February 16, Colorado Avalanche forward Steve Moore levelled Marcus Naslund, leaving the Vancouver star with a concussion and his Canucks teammates with other thoughts on their minds.

On March 3, the two teams met again, but with NHL commissioner Gary Bettman at the game, they stuck to hockey. That changed in their matchup five days later.

Emotions ran high as the March 8 game rapidly descended into a fight-filled affair. Moore dropped the gloves against Matt Cooke early on, but the pressure kept building until it exploded in the third period. Vancouver's Todd Bertuzzi delivered a blindside punch from behind to Moore, whom he then drove down into the ice surface. And with that, two lives were changed forever.

Moore suffered deep cuts to his face and three broken vertebrae. Nerves in his neck area were stretched. He would be plagued with post-concussion symptoms and amnesia. The NHL response was swift and firm, suspending Bertuzzi for the remainder of the season. Bertuzzi issued a heartfelt apology for the incident, but the story didn't end there. In August, he pleaded not guilty to a charge of assault causing bodily harm.

Opinions were divided about whether the matter belonged in the courts. Bertuzzi avoided a trial by agreeing to a plea bargain that saw him receive a sentence of community service. Moore has never played another game in the NHL. His February 2005 civil suit against Bertuzzi (and Canucks general manager Brian Burke and team member Brad May) was dismissed by a Colorado judge, who ruled that British Columbia was the proper jurisdiction for the matter.

Because of the NHL lockout, Bertuzzi's suspension was just 20 games, which at the time was tied for fourth-longest in league history. He lost nearly $1 million in salary and endorsements. He made repeated attempts to apologize to Moore in person.

BOB McKENZIE REMEMBERS

❝ What I remember the most about it is that it happened the night before the NHL trade deadline and we were at TSN for our wall-to-wall trade coverage. When I walked into the newsroom, someone said, "You've got to see what just happened." When I went over to look at it and I, thought to myself, "Oh my goodness, this is bad with a capital 'b.'" It was also one of those things that got bigger and bigger with each passing day, especially because of the injury to Moore. ❞

Jeff Vinnick/Getty Images

Todd Bertuzzi's face told a story of regret and sadness at his press conference following the Steve Moore incident.

THE LOCKOUT

European Road Trip!

Tim Boyle/Getty Images

JAMES**DUTHIE**

REMEMBERS

"It was the worst year of my career simply because I got into this business to talk about hockey games and players, not economics. Weeks would go by, nothing would change, so we were on TV every day literally talking about nothing. And there was really nothing you could do about it.

The NHL would say the deal gave them cost certainly and so it was worth it in the long run. I still think that the game paid a huge price for what happened. And it really wasn't that bad a deal for the Players Association. I think they've done a lot better than people thought they did, and the owners are still spending too much money, and you know that will never change. "

Storm clouds were on the horizon as the 2004 NHL season drew to a close. The existing Collective Bargaining Agreement (CBA) between NHL players and owners expired on September 15, and the prospects of an easy renegotiation looked far from likely.

On one side, the owners and NHL commissioner Gary Bettman were demanding cost certainty in the form of a salary cap. Players, led by union head Bob Goodenow, blamed the owners for escalating salaries and claimed they would never accept a cap. The lockout began on September 16, and for fans, the news just got worse and worse. Talks broke down and more than 300 NHL players accepted jobs with European teams. The two sides reconvened in December, providing fans a glimmer of hope. Goodenow and the National Hockey League Players' Association came forward with an offer, including a 24 percent rollback in salaries. The league rejected the offer, insisting that it needed some form of a cap. And the standoff continued.

There would be no more NHL hockey in 2004. And as the year drew to a close, the prospect of a settlement seemed distant indeed.

2005

TV TOP10 MOMENTS

1 Tiger Woods's chip from off the green on the 16th at Augusta makes a right turn and heads toward the hole. It pauses and goes in.

2 Commissioner Gary Bettman announces the NHL is cancelling the 2004-05 season when talks with players fail to produce a new collective bargaining agreement.

3 Baltimore's Rafael Palmeiro tells U.S. Congress he's never used steroids, "Period." He's suspended for steroid use five months later.

4 Pittsburgh's Sidney Crosby goes forehand, backhand, water bottle to beat Montreal's José Théodore for the shootout winner in his first game against a Canadian team.

5 Pittsburgh wins first pick — and the right to choose Sidney Crosby — in a post-lockout draft lottery in which every team has a shot at number one.

6 Double Dion! Canadian defenceman Dion Phaneuf ricochets off two Russians in one massive chain-reaction hit in the World Junior Championship gold-medal game.

7 The NHL's longest shootout ends when the Rangers' 15th shooter, Marek Malik, puts the puck between his legs and flips it by Washington goalie Olie Kolzig.

8 Steve Nash heads the ball to Amare Stoudemire, who slam-dunks it during the annual NBA Slam Dunk Contest.

9 Terrell Owens does sit-ups in his driveway during an impromptu press conference about his suspension by Philadelphia.

10 Mechanical engineer Brian Diesbourg of Belle River, Ontario, kicks a 50-yard field goal in the Wendy's Kick for a Million contest to claim the grand prize.

MADE IN CANADA

CANADIAN DREAM TEAM

World Juniors Team Steamrolls to Gold

For most experts, there was no question that the 2005 Canadian junior hockey team was the best ever. And they were hungry. Once the team to beat in the world junior tournament, Canada had gone without a gold medal since its run of seven straight titles ended in 1997. A year after getting beat by the Americans, the 2005 Canadian squad wasn't going to settle for silver, nor were they expected to.

The team entered the tournament as heavy favourites, at least partly because of the NHL lockout. A number of players who would have already made the jump to the highest level were available for the tournament. Rolling out a squad that included the likes of Dion Phaneuf, Jeff Carter, Patrice Bergeron, Corey Perry, Mike Richards, Sidney Crosby, Ryan Getzlaf and Shea Weber, the Canadian team outscored its opponents 32–5 during the preliminary round before dispensing with the Czech Republic 3–1 in the semifinal. The Russian team, World Junior Champion-

Jeff Vinnick/Getty Images

Future NHL stars Patrice Bergeron,

ship winners of gold in 2002 and 2003, awaited in the final.

But as they had done in the rest of the tournament, the Canadian team won going away, earning an easy 6–1 victory. Bergeron, Phaneuf and Carter were all named to the tournament all-star team. The 2005 championship would begin another run of consecutive world junior titles for Canada.

Sidney Crosby and Corey Perry celebrate gold for Canada.

TIGER WOODS INTENTIONALLY LANDS TOUGH CHIP ON 16TH AT AUGUSTA ABOVE THE HOLE WHERE BALL MAKES A RIGHT TURN AND HEADS TOWARDS THE CUP BEFORE PAUSING AND DROPPING IN.

❝You had this dogfight between Tiger Woods and Chris DiMarco. They both just birdied the 15th hole and Tiger had a one-shot lead. They get to 16 and DiMarco was in the centre of the green and Tiger hit one of the worst tee shots ever. He was lucky he hit it far enough that it went over the water, which left this impossible chip. And so everybody thought, "Here we go. All of sudden they're going to be all tied up again with a couple holes to play." And then the chip happens and we're in the media centre, looking at it on these big monitors on the other side of the course. That shot was just a perfect TV shot, zooming in on the ball and watching it pause there. And when it fell in, we could hear the roar inside the media centre from all the way across the golf course. It really was a defining moment for Tiger. It was just unbelievable because even though they went to a playoff, you kind of had a feeling that that was a huge moment. When something so big and drastic happens like that it almost seems like it's fate that he's going to win. ❞

GORD MILLER

REMEMBERS

❝That was a lockout year, so the NHL season was lost. Canada probably would have had eight or nine guys playing in the NHL that year. The defence on that team, with guys like Phaneuf and Weber, was incredible. The tournament was in Grand Forks, North Dakota but fans from southern Manitoba and southern Saskatchewan were in the stands in droves. Before the final, Brent Sutter wrote on the board: Their best players must feel pain. And I think it was Patrice Bergeron who hit Ovechkin in the first period and put him out with a shoulder injury. And 13 out of the 22 Team Canada players played at least one game in the NHL in the next year. ❞

TURNING POINT

ALL HAIL THE KID

NHL Draft Becomes "Sidney Crosby Sweepstakes"

Coming out of the lockout, the NHL's first order of business was to organize the draft lottery. Teams were given a weighted probability of having the first pick overall based on their results in previous seasons. In 2005, with a certain young Nova Scotian centre up for grabs, the event was quickly dubbed the "Sidney Crosby Sweepstakes."

The son of a former Montreal Canadiens draft pick, Crosby had been on the hockey radar since he was seven years old. An incredible talent with speed and awe-inspiring offensive gifts, his legend continued to grow. After he dominated every level of minor hockey, he was drafted first overall to the Quebec Major Junior Hockey League by the Rimouski Oceanic and proceeded to tally 135 points in his rookie season. He followed that with 168 points in 2004–05, guiding the Oceanic to the Memorial Cup final and solidifying his place as the number-one prospect for the NHL Entry Draft.

Pittsburgh won the lottery and it appeared to be a match made in heaven. Crosby would develop under the tutelage of owner and Hall-of-Fame teammate Mario Lemieux. With his 102-point rookie season, Crosby helped bring hockey back to the fore-front in Pittsburgh.

Dave Sandford/Getty Images

Showing maturity beyond his 18 years, Pittsburgh Penguin Sidney Crosby finished sixth in assists and points during his rookie NHL campaign.

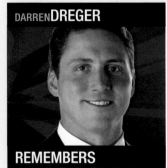

DARREN**DREGER**

REMEMBERS

"It changed the direction of the franchise. Prior to the lottery there were legitimate concerns over its survival. There certainly wasn't any concrete plan to build a new facility, which we see there is now. I recall watching the GMs' faces as it unfolded and I remember wondering how these men masked what had to be a combination of near torture mixed with the endless possibilities that would come with winning. It was nothing short of a riveting TV experience. "

STEVE NASH WINS NBA MVP

Edges Out Shaquille O'Neal for Award

In 2005, Steve Nash accomplished one of the most unlikely feats for any Canadian athlete. A six-foot-three point guard from Victoria, B.C., Nash put together the season of a lifetime in his first year with the Phoenix Suns and edged out none other than Shaquille O'Neal for the NBA MVP Award.

Despite O'Neal's huge popularity, and impressive seasons by other NBA superstars, Nash's win brought little controversy. An astounding passer with unparalleled court vision, he led the league in assists by a margin of two and a half helpers per game, guiding an unheralded Suns team to a league-leading 110 points-per-game average and increasing the team's win total to 62 from 29 a year earlier.

Nash became just the fourth point guard to win the award, after Magic Johnson, Oscar Robertson and Bob Cousy. And he made Canadians proud, not just for his accomplishment, but for the humility with which he handled it.

"I definitely won this award because of my role on this team," he said after the announcement. "I didn't win this award because I'm overpowering people or dominating the game with physical ability."

Elsa/Getty Images

The 6-foot-3 Nash joined Allen Iverson as the only MVP winners in more than 40 years to measure less than 6-foot-6 in height.

JACK**ARMSTRONG**

REMEMBERS

❝ For a Phoenix team coached by Mike Dantoni, Nash was the perfect player. He was a guy who was fully able to lock into the talent around him and know what buttons to push to make everyone around him that much better. He was a throwback to Bob Cousy, and able to make incredible decisions at an amazingly quick speed.

For people to see a guy like that doing what he did, he was carrying on a tradition of Cousy, Magic Johnson and John Stockton. Fans appreciated him and his MVP win gave players who are maybe a little smaller the belief that they can still be impact players. When he won, as a basketball person, I was not surprised. There's always "the sizzle factor" vs. "the substance factor," and Steve Nash's game has both. He's incredibly entertaining and his level of basketball intellect is off the charts. He gave a lot of young Canadian players someone to model themselves after. ❞

TSN THAT'S HOCKEY

NHL ARENAS REMAIN DARK

Season Cancelled

Bruce Bennett/Getty Images

When NHL commissioner Gary Bettman announced the cancellation of the 2004 season, he ensured there would be no Stanley Cup champion for the first time since 1919, when the final was called off due to a flu epidemic.

RAY FERRARO

REMEMBERS

As 2005 rolled on, there was a glaring absence on the professional sports landscape: the NHL. The lockout, which had begun in September 2004, showed little sign of ending, and efforts by the NHL Players' Association and owners didn't appear to hold much promise. At its core, the dispute was over a salary cap, something the owners wanted but the players didn't.

The days and weeks dragged on with no compromise, and hope among hockey fans and negotiators diminished. As the calendar hit mid-February, there was only one move left to make. On February 16, NHL commissioner Gary

Bettman announced the formal cancellation of play for the 2004–05 season. Despite the acrimony on display, many fans were still incredulous, and rightfully so. It was the first-ever full-season cancellation — including a championship — of a major sport.

But with the summer looming and another season in jeopardy, talks resumed with a hint of optimism. After months of intense negotiating, the worst crisis in NHL history was finally solved on July 13. With some controversy, the NHL and NHLPA had agreed to a new Collective Bargaining Agreement. The players accepted a cap after all. The game was

" I don't think anybody believed it would last all year. I went on strike in '92 and that was 10 days. There was a lockout a few years later where we lost half a season, and as a player, you start getting scared a little bit. The NHL Players Association totally misjudged two things: 1) was the resolve of the owners this time around and 2) was that they felt the players' salaries would allow them to wait out the lockout for a long period of time. The salary stuff became a weakness, because the players were sitting around in early January and going, "Wait a minute, I make $3 million. I've already lost a million and a half." Certain players, of course, make it back tenfold. Others don't come back from these lockouts. The game moves past them. I don't know how successful for both sides it all was. Coming right out of the lockout, everybody thought the players got crushed on this deal. But they seem to be doing fine. "

back for the 2005–06 season, but it wasn't quite the same. The salary cap meant that competition for top-level free agents was open to small-market teams. Players contributed to a competition committee, which helped bring changes into the game. Two-line passes were legal, obstruction was down, scoring was up. A shootout system was implemented to settle regular-season tie games. Shutouts were rare, comebacks were commonplace and impenetrable neutral-zone traps were not. Most importantly, the NHL was back in action.

With a new deal signed, union head Bob Goodenow resigned, ending his 15-year tenure as the players' representative.

Brad White/Getty Images

DAVE RANDORF

REMEMBERS

BRIAN DIESBOURG KICKS A 50-YARD FIELD GOAL IN WENDY'S KICK FOR A MILLION CONTEST TO CLAIM THE GRAND PRIZE.

❝ Brian is a guy who's never played football, never even been to a football game. He plays men's soccer, so he could kick a ball. So we get out there and he kicks the 20-yarder and it's not a bad kick (about two feet wide to the right). He moves back to the 30. Again, pretty good kick, lots of leg, plenty of distance, about two feet wide to the right. He heads back to the 40, and now he's got the attention of 40,000 people and he nails his 40-yarder, lots of leg and it's about two feet wide—to the right. I'm the guy hosting the whole thing at mid-field standing beside Brian, Matt Dunigan, Chris Schultz and Jock Climie and we're looking at each other and thinking the same thing, "He just might do this!" All of a sudden, this moment's got a bit of a buzz. It's halftime and nobody has left their seats. So I have to say, on live TV, "OK, well we've got one kick left from 50 yards. We're gonna kick this kick right after the commercial break."

So now, I'm standing there at mid-field, in a jam-packed stadium, right beside Brian, and it's kind of eerie because it feels like we're alone in a room together, and I'm trying not to look at him and he's definitely not looking at me. He's looking straight ahead at the uprights. The two-minute break seemed like 20 minutes. I couldn't hold myself back. I kind of nudged up to him and said, "You know, you just miss it about two feet to the right every time," and he says, " I know!" and I said, "OK!" and backed away. So, we came back and I said, "OK, let's do it. One kick. Fifty yards. A million bucks." And he nailed it, right down the pipes. It wasn't wide, right, it couldn't have been more down the middle, and I've never heard such a roar for such an unlikely hero. Both teams, the Tiger Cats and the Argos, came flying out of the tunnels and just buried this guy. They couldn't believe it either. And it wasn't even truly a sports moment because it didn't take place in a game or an official event of any kind. It ran not only on TSN for about two weeks, but all across North America and on sports highlights reels in Europe. It was a moment, honestly, that we will never forget. Field goal kickers could not believe that this guy kicked a 50-yard field goal out of nowhere. The most unlikely guy in the world hit the jackpot. It was front page of two national, daily papers. It was completely unexpected . . . hilarious, and made everybody stand up and cheer. ❞

2006

CINDY KLASSEN'S MEDAL HAUL

Ties Olympic Record for Podium Finishes

Tim Boyle/Getty Images

Cindy Klassen won the Lou Marsh Trophy as Canada's athlete of the year.

Canada won an unprecedented 24 medals at the Turin 2006 Olympic Winter Games. Leading the way was speed skater Cindy Klassen, who did something no other Canadian athlete ever had. But for a bit of adversity, it might never have happened.

Klassen only took up speed skating after the devastating disappointment of being cut from the 1998 Canadian women's hockey team. An elite hockey player throughout her youth, her speed skating coaches initially complained that her skating style didn't suit the sport. But the hard-working Klassen fell in love with the challenge of individual competition. Meanwhile, her ever-improving times offered ample proof of her talent. A bronze medallist at the Salt Lake City 2002 Olympic Winter Games, Klassen was expected to reach the podium in Turin in four races. And she did not disappoint, capturing one bronze and two silver medals for her performances in the 3000 metres, 1000 metres and Team Pursuit. In her best distance, the 1500 metres, Klassen beat teammate Kristina Groves by more than a second to capture gold.

In her last race, the 5000 metres, even Klassen herself didn't expect to finish in the top three. But the Manitoba native brought home the bronze, finishing less than a minute behind fellow Canadian Clara Hughes, who won gold. With her five-medal performance, Klassen tied Eric Heiden's 1980 record for speed skating medals in a single Olympic Games and shattered the previous Canadian record of three medals set in 1984 by Gaétan Boucher. With six total medals to her name, she is Canada's most decorated Olympic athlete.

JENNIFER HEDGER REMEMBERS

❝ Cindy Klassen is such an interesting athlete because she is somebody who completely dominates her sport, and yet you could not meet a more humble person. It's a rare mix, but it is also so very Canadian for an athlete to have that delicate balance. But she had it in spades. I remember watching her and there was really no question in my mind whether or not she was going to break the medals record. As far as what it meant for the country, Cindy Klassen allowed us to breathe a big sigh of relief and give thanks that this woman was competing for our country, both because of her results and the fact that she is just such a classy individual. ❞

GUSHUE GRABS GOLD

Canadian Curler Rules Olympic Rings

Despite his young age, by the time Brad Gushue arrived at the Olympic Winter Games in Turin, he already had a long and impressive resumé in the curling world. The 25-year-old Newfoundlander was a six-time provincial junior champion, a national and world junior champion in 2001 and had three solid Brier showings in 2003, 2004 and 2005.

With his sights set on qualifying to represent Canada at the 2006 Winter Games, in 2005 Gushue made a surprising move, inviting former world champion and New Brunswick resident Russ Howard to join his rink as a fifth player. But Howard would assume a more integral role when second Mike Adams stepped aside to let Howard take his shots. In order to take full advantage of the 49-year-old's experience, Gushue himself shared some of his duties as skip. He had Howard call the games as a skip would but always retained the right to make the final decision. Whatever doubts people had about the personnel change, it paid off big time at the Olympic trials.

In Turin, Gushue and company faltered early on and had to rely on wins in their final two games just to make the semi-finals. But once they did, they made no mistakes, defeating the U.S. 11–5 before facing Finland for the gold. What was a very tight game broke open in the sixth end when Canada took advantage of Finnish errors to score six. With Canada holding a sizeable 10–4 advantage, Finnish skip Markku Uusipaavalniemi conceded defeat with two ends remaining.

It was Canada's first-ever men's curling gold after disappointing losses in 1998 and 2002. Gushue was overjoyed. His first call was to his mother, who was recovering from cancer treatments in Newfoundland. Howard turned 50 during the games and is the oldest Canadian gold medallist in Winter Olympics history. Gushue and his teammates were the first Newfoundlanders ever to win gold. The province officially allowed the closure of all schools at noon on the day of the final so that kids and teachers could go home to watch.

Clive Rose/Getty Images

Brad Gushue attained instant celebrity in Canada after his gold medal performance. In addition, he and his teammates were invested into the Order of Newfoundland and Labrador and had a new road in St. John's renamed Team Gushue Highway.

LINDA**MOORE**

REMEMBERS

❝ What was really fantastic about those Olympic Games is how they recovered from difficult losses in the round robin, won their last two games and then won the semifinals and finals. The poise they showed, as well as the mental skills to recover their focus and go on to win gold, was something that we'll always look at as a wonderful achievement. ❞

MADE IN CANADA

BUCK**MARTINEZ**

REMEMBERS

" When Justin Morneau came into the 2006 season he was a 25-year-old guy and starting to get his man strength, and his man strength took over. It allowed him to just take it further knowing that he didn't have to try to generate power, that he had enough power there already. But the team around him was pretty good as well. I think that's the one thing you have to have if you're going to be a star player: you need to have complementary players around you. They had other guys that helped complement his MVP skills. That was important for him. He also began to understand that he had a responsibility to his teammates to be prepared and be the leader both in the game itself and in the character that he represents himself with. He is truly what it means to be an MVP: he is a leader, he is prepared, he is a batter and he's a marvelous player. He reflects all the Canadian attributes that I've come to know in my time in Toronto. He's respectful of his teammates, he's respectful of the game, he understands the importance of relating to the fans and he wants to represent himself, his family and his country. "

With 32 dingers in his MVP season, Justin Morneau was the first Minnesota Twin to hit the 30-home-run mark since 1987.

JUSTIN MORNEAU WINS AL MVP

Becomes Second Canadian to Win a League MVP Award

It's a long way from New Westminster, B.C., to the big leagues. In 2003, Justin Morneau made the jump to the majors. In 2006, he proved he not only belonged, but was one of the best players in the game.

Morneau's contribution to the Minnesota Twins that year is easy to measure. A slow start to the 2006 Major League Baseball season saw the team's record standing at 24–28 at the end of May. In June, Morneau batted .364 with 10 home runs, leading the Twins to a 19–7 record for the month and back into the hunt for the American League Central Division title. If there were any weaknesses in the left-handed batter's swing, they

had disappeared, as he hit .315 with 13 home runs against lefties for the year. He finished the season hitting .321 with 34 homers and 130 RBIs, was instrumental in the Twins' AL Central title and beat out Derek Jeter of the New York Yankees and David Ortiz of the Boston Red Sox for the MVP honour. The Twins lost to the Oakland A's in the AL Division Series.

With a breakout year, the 25-year old became only the second Canadian to be named the league MVP, joining his boyhood idol Larry Walker in a very exclusive Canadian club. "He's the player that all Canadian position players are measured up against," Morneau said of Walker upon receiving the award.

John Reid III/MLB Photos via Getty Images

HEAVY-HEARTED TIGER MANAGES MAJOR VICTORIES

Still Crushed by Loss of Dad

Woods said his British Open victory at Royal Liverpool would have made his father, Earl, very proud because of the way he managed the golf course. Over four days at the treacherous track, he was in just three bunkers.

Doug Benc/Getty Images

CORY WORON REMEMBERS

" When his dad passed and he took all the time off before he came back to Winged Foot, the big question was: "How is Tiger going to play?" And he missed the cut for the first time in a major as a pro. It was a huge blow professionally, but you knew that he was battling with himself. I mean, it was a struggle for him to be there. His job, everyday, every second on the golf course, is a reminder of his dad. Then he wins the British Open and there's that hug that he had with Steve Williams at the end. And like he said, it just came pouring out of him. It was such a cathartic moment. And we all know what he did for the rest of that year, I mean, six consecutive PGA Tour victories and another major championship. It was almost like when he found a way to win after his father died he had a different purpose, and it's funny because he's one of the most focused and intense competitors that you've ever seen. But, it just seemed like he had a different way to channel that now, and I think it made him stronger as a person and obviously stronger as a player for the rest of that season. **"**

Tiger Woods won eight PGA tournaments in 2006, including six in a row and two majors. But for Tiger, 2006 was not a year for celebration.

On May 3, his father, Earl Woods, passed away after a long battle with cancer. The world's greatest golfer lost more than just a dad that day. For Tiger, he was best friend, mentor, coach, teacher or, as Tiger himself summed up, "basically everything."

After a nine-week layoff following his father's death, Woods returned to the competitive golf world for the U.S. Open at Winged Foot. His heart was heavy and his head was clearly not where it needed to be. The result: his first missed cut in a major as a professional. But a tie for second three weeks later at the Western Open showed he had cleaned the rust off his game. And at the British Open a week later, the old Tiger was back. He was the model of course management (he hit driver just once all week), putting with incredible accuracy as he recorded a stunning -18 at Royal Liverpool to capture his first major without his father, and the 11th of his career. Following the last putt, he broke down in tears, realizing his dad would never see him win again.

From July on, Woods didn't lose a tournament he entered, ripping off six consecutive victories, including the PGA Championship (with another -18 performance) and the 50th win of his career.

TURNING POINT

ZINEDINE ZIDANE LOSES THEN USES HEAD

Head-butt Expulsion Costs France World Cup

It was one of the most shocking incidents in sports. Veteran midfielder Zinedine Zidane had been France's best player through the group and knockout stages of the 2006 World Cup. In the final against arch-rival Italy, he scored their only goal as the two teams entered extra time in a 1–1 tie. In the 110th minute of the game, as Zidane and Italian defender Marco Materazzi jogged back up the pitch, the two players exchanged words after Materazzi appeared to grab Zidane's jersey. Initially, Zidane walked away, but then he stopped suddenly, turned and head-butted Materazzi in the chest, sending him to the ground. The officials conferred for a short time before referee Horacio Elizondo issued Zidane a red card, removing the star from the game.

Shock turned to agony for the French football fans as Italy went on to win 5–3 in penalty kicks, denying France the World Cup. With a team-leading three goals in the tournament, Zidane would surely have taken a penalty kick for his country. It was widely thought that the incident turned the tide for Italy.

Many theories were postulated over what Materazzi said to provoke Zidane. In the end, the Italian player admitted to insulting Zidane's sister, though he claimed he didn't even know the French player had one. Despite the incident, Zidane was awarded the Golden Ball as the best player in the tournament. In the weeks that followed, the incident took on a life of its own. A song entitled "Coup de Boule," or "Head-butt," written and performed by Sébastien and Emmanuel Lipszyc, climbed to number one on French and Belgian singles charts and reached number two in Italy.

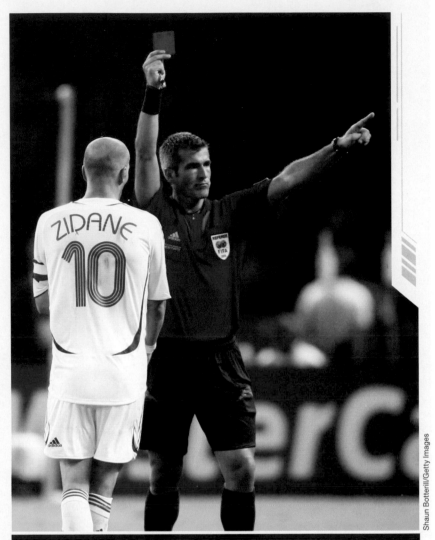

Shaun Botterill/Getty Images

One of the world's greatest footballers, France's Zinedine Zidane was also one of the most emotional. He is one of only two players to be issued a red card in two separate World Cups, and one of just four to be red-carded in a final.

DAN O'TOOLE REMEMBERS

❝ Zidane was one of the greatest soccer players of all time and a head-butt is what he'll be remembered for. No one could understand why a guy would do this on that big of a stage. It's the World Cup final and you let someone get under your skin like that. It's hard to comprehend. And then his team ends up losing in a shootout — a shootout that he can't take part in because he's been kicked out of the game. It will go down as one of the most viewed and discussed World Cup highlights of all time. ❞

OVER THE MOON

Damon Allen Breaks Warren Moon's Record for Passing Yardage

After 22 years expertly plying his trade as a CFL quarterback, 43-year-old Toronto Argonaut Damon Allen achieved truly legendary status with a short shovel pass to Arland Bruce III for a 29-yard touchdown. With the completion, Allen passed Warren Moon to become professional football's all-time leading passer.

Allen finished the game — a 40–6 win over Hamilton in the Labour Day Classic — with a career total of 70,596 yards, 43 more than the 70,553 Moon amassed while playing in both the CFL and NFL.

Following the record-breaking completion, the game was stopped for a short ceremony to honour the mark. The ball was presented to Allen by CFL commissioner Tom Wright, Argonauts co-owners David Cynamon and Howard Sokolowski and former NFL head coach Steve Mariucci, who was also Allen's quarterback coach during his college career at California State University, Fullerton.

A veteran of six CFL teams, Allen retired from the Argonauts in 2007 holding the career CFL marks for passing yards, passing touchdowns, pass attempts, pass completions and rushing yards by a quarterback (and third in all-time rushing by any player). The four-time Grey Cup winner and brother of NFL Hall of Famer Marcus Allen, was the league's Most Outstanding Player in 2005 and a two-time Grey Cup Most Valuable Player (1993, 2004).

In college, Allen was also a top-level baseball player. He helped lead the Cal State Fullerton Titans to a College World Series title in 1984 and was drafted by the Detroit Tigers in the seventh round that year.

John Sokolowski

Damon Allen holds up the game ball in acknowledgement of the crowd at Ivor Wynne Stadium in Hamilton after breaking the all-time professional passing record.

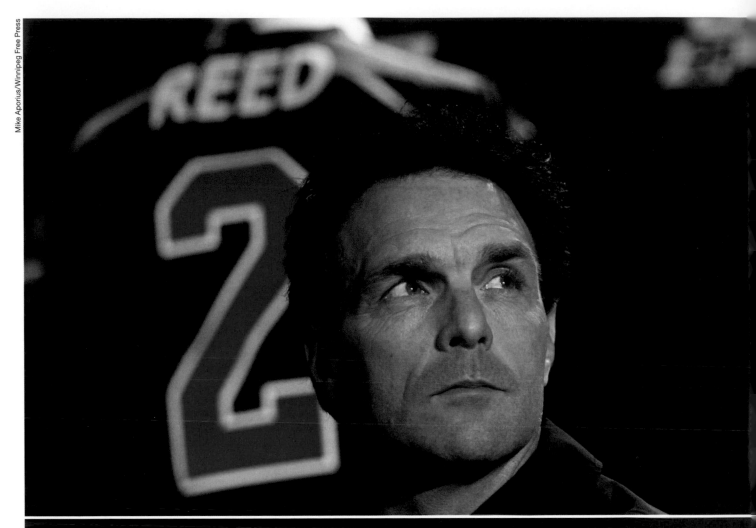

The greatest ever: No. 1 player Doug Flutie addresses the media at the press conference announcing TSN's Top 50 festivities in Winnipeg.

Mike Aporius/Winnipeg Free Press

CFL TOP 50

1. Doug Flutie, Quarterback
2. George Reed, Running Back
3. Jackie Parker, QB/RB/DB
4. Mike Pringle, Running Back
5. Warren Moon, Quarterback
6. Garney Henley, Defensive Back/Receiver
7. Ron Lancaster, Quarterback
8. Russ Jackson, Quarterback
9. Wayne Harris Sr., Linebacker
10. Allen Pitts, Receiver
11. Dan Kepley, Linebacker
12. John Helton, Defensive Lineman
13. Hal Patterson, Receiver/Defensive Back

14. Damon Allen, Quarterback
15. Milt Stegall, Receiver
16. Willie Pless, Linebacker
17. John Barrow, Defensive/Offensive Lineman
18. Tony Gabriel, Receiver
19. Johnny Bright, Running Back
20. Brian Kelly, Receiver
21. James Parker, Defensive Lineman /Linebacker
22. Chris Walby, Offensive Lineman
23. Less Browne, Defensive Back
24. Dave Fennell, Defensive Lineman
25. Henry (Gizmo) Williams, Special Teams
26. Sam Etcheverry, Quarterback

A WHO'S WHO OF CANADIAN FOOTBALL GREATS

TSN Top 50 CFL Players

Players from the modern era, during the 2006 Grey Cup

From Doug Flutie to George Reed to Jackie Parker to hundreds of others, the CFL has been blessed with some of the finest football players ever to lace up cleats. To honour the rich and storied history of the league, in 2006 TSN initiated the Top 50 CFL Players program to generate debate and recognize the players who shaped the game. Working with the league, TSN assembled a 60-member independent expert panel consisting of media, former players, coaches, broadcasters and football executives. Panellists were provided with 185 player candidates, including 119 players elected to the Canadian Football Hall of Fame on the basis of performance since 1945 and 66 others identified during months of research and consultation.

Each panellist voted for his or her own top 50, comparing players based on the totality of their on-field contributions. Each voter was required to include at least one quarterback, two running backs, four receivers, five offensive linemen, one punter (or punter/kicker), one kicker (or kicker/punter), four defensive linemen, three linebackers and five defensive backs, for a total of 26 players representing every position. There were no restrictions on the remaining 24 choices.

The result is a list of the top 50 CFL players who have left their mark on the history of Canadian football.

27. **Tommy Joe Coffey**, Receiver/Kicker
28. **Grover Covington**, Defensive Lineman
29. **Leo Lewis**, Running Back
30. **Lui Passaglia**, Kicker/Punter
31. **Michael (Pinball) Clemons**, Special Teams/Running Back/Receiver
32. **Roger Aldag**, Offensive Lineman
33. **Dickie Harris**, Defensive Back
34. **Normie Kwong**, Running Back
35. **Marv Luster**, Defensive Back/Receiver
36. **Ray Elgaard**, Receiver
37. **Angelo Mosca**, Defensive Lineman
38. **Larry Highbaugh**, Defensive Back

39. **Matt Dunigan**, Quarterback
40. **Joe Montford**, Defensive Lineman
41. **Kaye Vaughan**, Offensive/Defensive Lineman
42. **Mervyn Fernandez**, Receiver
43. **Bill Baker**, Defensive Lineman
44. **Danny Bass**, Linebacker
45. **Terry Vaughn**, Receiver
46. **Joe Krol**, Running Back
47. **Tom Clements**, Quarterback
48. **Rollie Miles**, Defensive Back /Running Back /Linebacker
49. **Bill Frank**, Offensive Lineman
50. **Darren Flutie**, Receiver

2007

BARRY BONDS SETS HR RECORD

Is Later Charged With Perjury

It was a bombshell and Major League Baseball's worst nightmare. The release of the Mitchell Report on the use of steroids in baseball established that players on every club in the game had been involved in using performance-enhancing drugs at some time in their careers. According to U.S. Senator George Mitchell, there was plenty of blame to go around. "Everyone involved in baseball over the past two decades," Mitchell said, "commissioners, club officials, the players association, the players, shares to some extent the responsibility for the Steroids Era."

Amid this controversy, San Francisco Giant Barry Bonds was living what should have been the culmination of a Hall of Fame career as he was poised to break Henry Aaron's career home run record, perhaps the most hallowed mark in all of sports. But Bonds was front and centre in the steroid controversy and had been since it was learned he testified before the BALCO steroid probe. His march toward the all-time record was badly tainted in the eyes of fans.

At AT&T Park in San Francisco, though, Giants fans couldn't get enough of Bonds and his pursuit of the record. And that's where he was on the evening of August 7, tied with Aaron with 755 home runs to his name, facing the Washington Nationals' Mike Bacsik. At 8:51 PM, he hit a fastball 435 feet into the night and over the wall in right-centre field. It was number 756. Bonds dropped his bat and threw his arms in the air

Rich Pilling/MLB Photos via Getty Images

Over his career, Barry Bonds hit a home run roughly every 13 at bats, third best in major-league history.

as thousands of flashbulbs accompanied a very clear and emphatic roar from the sell-out crowd. Fireworks lit up the Bay outside the stadium as Bonds circled the bases. He was mobbed by his family and teammates before making a short speech that finished with a thank you to his father. Aaron was not at the game, but delivered a pre-recorded congratulatory message played on the ballpark's video screen in center field.

Bonds finished the year with 28 home runs, to put his career total — and baseball's new home run record — at 762. But his celebration was to be short-lived. Just a couple of months after the season, on December 7, he was in a San Francisco courtroom pleading not guilty to five charges of perjury and obstruction of justice connected to grand jury testimony he gave about the steroid issue in 2003.

MICHAEL LANDSBERG REMEMBERS

❝ I think that in some ways his arrogance insulated him and was protection for him. He really believed that he was above the law and above the rules. Love the record, don't love the man. I look at Bonds and try to look beyond his weaknesses and say, "You've got to admire a guy for being able to hit that many home runs." End of the story. ❞

COMING TO AMERICA
David Beckham Expands Universe with Galaxy

The story broke on January 12, receiving just about as much play in entertainment news as it did in sports. The world's most recognized athlete, David Beckham, had signed the richest contract in the history of American team sports — five years, $250 million — to play for the Los Angeles Galaxy of Major League Soccer. The team and the league were banking on the former Manchester United and Real Madrid hotshot to provide an instant boost for the sport, much as Brazil's Pelé had for the defunct North American Soccer League in the 1970s.

Beckham's star power showed itself from the start. The Galaxy sold a record 250,000 jerseys even before he was officially introduced as a league member.

Still, theories would abound as to why Beckham would come to North America. Already fabulously wealthy, he was competing against the very best in the sport in Europe. Asked point-blank, Beckham responded that he felt it was time for a change. "I played at the highest level for 15 years," he said, "and now I think that I need another challenge."

Despite flashes of brilliance during his first season, Beckham suffered a sprained ligament in just his second month with the team. The Galaxy were eliminated from playoff contention with a 1–0 loss to the Chicago Fire in the team's final game of the season.

In 2008, Beckham led the Galaxy with 10 assists, but the team finished near the bottom of the standings. He spent the 2009 off-season playing with AC Milan, on loan. Speculation was that the all-world midfielder wished to retain match fitness to possibly represent England in the 2010 World Cup.

Chad Buchanan/Getty Images

David Beckham scored on a free kick in his first game with the Los Angeles Galaxy.

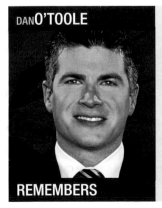

DAN O'TOOLE
REMEMBERS

" In essence, this was the MLS putting a neon sign above their league saying, "We're for real now." They knew it was a massive figure and it would get attention. They knew the profile that David Beckham already had in Europe and across North America. And by bringing him here, signing him to a contract like that, you get every headline in the world of sports. The L.A. Galaxy, wherever they played, they sold out, and that means people are watching a sport that they aren't really used to seeing in North America. So, if they could get these viewers to stick around and actually watch games that David Beckham wasn't in, then there was mission accomplished. And they got a national TV deal, ESPN was broadcasting games that David Beckham was playing in, his introduction news conference in L.A. was broadcast live. By signing that contract, they launched David Beckham into a stratosphere that only a few athletes have attained in modern-day sports. There's high-profile, rich athletes, and then there's the next level. And Tiger Woods and David Beckham are two that have reached that other level. And that contract is what put David Beckham there. "

2008

Clive Brunskill/Getty Images

Julian Finney/Getty Images

Rafael Nadal's victory in the Wimbledon final ended Roger Federer's streak of 65 consecutive grass-court wins.

WIMBLEDON MARATHON

Nadal Outlasts Federer in Epic Battle

From the outset it had the potential to be a great final. Number-one seed Roger Federer, seeking a record-tying sixth-consecutive Wimbledon title, taking on number-two Rafael Nadal for the third consecutive year. The rivalry had been dominated by Federer, except at the French Open, where Nadal was a four-time winner. With the win, Federer would creep even closer to Pete Sampras's all-time record of 14 Grand Slam titles. Nadal, a young Spaniard with unbelievable speed and power, was eager to prove he could beat his rival on a surface other than clay.

Prior to the final, Nadal shook hands with Manuel Santana, the 1966 champion and the last Spanish player to win the men's singles final.

His countryman's magic seemed to rub off as Nadal immediately took the upper hand. He won the first set 6–4 in less than an hour and took the second by the same score, despite trailing 4–1 at one point in the set. Perhaps aided by a rain delay that slowed the set, Federer eked out a 7–5 tie-break win in the third set and did the same in an almost identical fourth. This time, Nadal took a 5–2 tie-break lead but Federer came back to win 10–8 and force a fifth set.

In the fifth, the back-and-forth play continued until Nadal finally triumphed 9–7 at 9:16 PM. The marathon of heart-stopping tennis was over. Nadal climbed into the crowd to meet his family and celebrate and would later say: "It's impossible to explain what I felt when I won . . . I never thought I could win, but to do so is a dream."

Rain delayed the match an hour and a half and pushed it over six hours, but the playing time alone of four hours and 48 minutes made it the longest final match in Wimbledon history. It was hailed by former champion and commentator John McEnroe as "the greatest match I have ever seen."

RECEIVER JASON TUCKER SUFFERS WHAT WOULD BE A CAREER-ENDING NECK INJURY JULY 26 VS. HAMILTON BUT MAKES AN EMOTIONAL RETURN TO EDMONTON FIVE DAYS LATER.

❝ The Eskimos were flat in the first game back home vs. the B.C. Lions. Jason Tucker surprises them by showing up in the dressing room. Then comes this play where quarterback Ricky Ray goes over the middle to Kamau Peterson, who goes up in the air to catch the ball and gets drilled by Otis Floyd. Peterson does great to hang onto the football, but you think this could be another serious injury. But it's Floyd who gets up slowly. Peterson springs to his feet and lifts up his jersey to reveal Tucker's No. 83 on a t-shirt underneath. The whole place explodes, the face of the game changes and Edmonton takes off from there to win. ❞

Walter Tychnowicz/Canadian Press

Kamau Peterson displayed intense emotion in tribute to injured friend and teammate Jason Tucker, who was at the game against the B.C. Lions

PLAYING ON AN INJURED LEG, TIGER WOODS TAKES 90 HOLES TO FINALLY DEFEAT FAN-FAVOURITE ROCCO MEDIATE AT THE U.S. OPEN.

❝ I remember hunkering down for the 18-hole play-off on Monday with Rocco and Tiger and firmly rooting for Rocco. Not only was he an enormous underdog, here was this 46-year-old guy who looked like he couldn't beat you in a foot race. I was also very skeptical and almost annoyed with the American media going on and on about Tiger and this leg, not because of anything Tiger did or said, but more because of the way they were just jumping on this story. But as the round went on and Tiger was hobbling around, I was starting to think to myself, "It looks as though he's really struggling." I felt a bit sheepish in the end when I found out that he basically was playing on a broken leg. But if there was ever going to be a defining tournament for Tiger Woods, that arguably was it. You can be the best golfer in the world, but there's an intangible competition factor that only so many people have, and Tiger Woods, obviously, has it. ❞

THE KINGS OF BEIJING

Usain Bolt and Michael Phelps Rule

After Usain Bolt won the 200 metres, "Happy Birthday" was played on the stadium's sound system. At midnight, it would be his 22nd birthday.

Ezra Shaw/Getty Images

Beijing may have been a controversial choice to host the Olympic Summer Games given the international outcry against China over human rights, but there was no disputing two of the finest athletic performances ever seen. Eight gold medals for American swimmer Michael Phelps made him the story of the Games; 100 lightning-fast metres from Jamaican sprinter Usain Bolt made him the undisputed king.

Coming into the Games, expectations for Phelps were through the roof. How could they not be? With six gold and two bronze medals from the Athens 2004 Olympic Summer Games and seven gold medals from

the 2007 World Championships, he had a realistic chance to surpass the record seven golds earned by American Mark Spitz at the 1972 Summer Games.

Beginning with a gold medal and a world record in the 400-metre individual medley on August 10, Phelps was the focus of world attention over the seven days as he rolled off seven more gold medals and, incredibly, seven more world records. The closest call came in the 100-metre butterfly, when he edged out Serbian Milorad Cavic by 1/100th of a second. Upon winning his eighth gold medal — swimming a record time in his butterfly leg of the 4 x 100 metre medley relay — Phelps summed

After American swimmer Michael Phelps captured his eighth gold medal, the man whose record he took, Mark Spitz, called him "the greatest racer who ever walked the planet."

MICHAEL**LANDSBERG**

REMEMBERS

❝ Usain Bolt and Michael Phelps, no question, are the defining athletes of the 2008 Summer Games, and maybe, just maybe, the defining athletes in the last 50 years in the Olympic Games.

Bolt: He wins the 100 metres in world-record time and doesn't appear to be trying. Usain Bolt runs faster than anyone in history in the 100 metres and the 200 metres. That to me says that he was the star of the Games and the star of the history of the Games.

Phelps: Imagine how many things Michael Phelps had to do perfectly: how many starts, how many turns, how many strokes! ❞

up his performance: "Records are always made to be broken no matter what they are . . . Anybody can do anything that they set their mind to."

Usain Bolt must have been listening.

The Jamaican sprinter had been on the radar since his win at the 2002 World Junior Championship and captured serious attention with a world-record 100-metre time of 9.72 seconds at the 2008 World Championship. It all paled in comparison to his performance in Beijing. Untouchable through the early heats, Bolt incredibly appeared to let up over the last 25 metres of the final to begin his celebration but nonetheless grabbed gold in

a world-record time of 9.69 seconds. The sprinter was criticized by some for what appeared to be showboating. Bolt denied this, saying he was "just happy" and turned his attention to the 200-metre race, where he would attempt to equal Carl Lewis's rare double gold in the events. There was no letting up in this event, as he pushed through to the finish line in a new world-record time of 19.30 seconds. Two days later, he ran the third leg in the 4 x 100 metre relay, leading his Jamaican team to a world record and the gold medal. After his wins, Bolt donated $50,000 to the children affected by the 2008 earthquake in China.

PHOTO CREDITS

FRONT COVER (from left to right):
Paul Bereswill/Hockey Hall of Fame; Rick Stewart/Getty Images Sport; Jeff Vinnick/Getty Images; David Boily/The Canadian Press

BACK COVER (from left to right):
Jeff Vinnick/hockeycanada.ca; Romeo Gacad/AFP/Getty Images; Elsa/Getty Images; Paul Bereswill/Hockey Hall of Fame